To: Analese

101 Author Tips

Creating a Successful Book Campaign

LifeTips Book Series

P.J. Campbell
LifeTips Publishing Expert Guru

Such a pleasure to have you in Events this Summer. I wish you the very best for the future! Write On, Write Now,

P.J.

Contents

A Note From the Editor

Writing a book is a huge accomplishment, but many of us overlook the fact that a written work has to somehow get into the hands of the readers it seeks to inspire and entertain. I can remember starting out as a creative writing student in college, eager to place myself in the romanticized image of the "struggling artist." Once I began studying the book publishing process, however, I realized that being a writer is about way more than the writing process itself and that authorhood doesn't have to conjure images of ramen noodles, empty coffee cups, and full ashtrays. I realized that writers can actually make money by doing what they love. As I delved further into the book publishing world, I also realized that a book's success has a lot to do with its author's willingness to get out and sell it.

In *101 Author Tips: Creating a Successful Book Campaign*, P.J. Campbell reminds aspiring authors that, once your book is written and published, you're nowhere near finished with it—that aside from being your labor of love, a book is a commodity that should pay the bills. Many of us assume that the publisher takes care of the actual selling of a book, but this is only partly true. P.J. teaches us that, while most publishers do have a hand in the promotion of their books, there are myriad steps that authors can take to complement and enhance these efforts.

The tips in this book will help aspiring or published authors navigate the post-publication process and exhaust what must be nearly every possible avenue of self-promotion and marketing in order to make their creativity pay off.

Holly Bauer, Editor

A Note from the Author

About fifteen years ago, I set out to discover what it would take to become a successful author.

I worked in an independent bookstore for almost two years as a General Manager and Director of Events, then I took the position of Events Manager for a major New York publisher. Through my experience and in my present position as the Director of Events, I have developed a keen sense of how an author can achieve a winning book campaign. It includes publicizing, marketing, and positioning both who you are as the author and what your book is about, plus one other essential ingredient: PASSION.

"101 Author Tips has essential information and valuable tips for inquisitive authors who are eager to know the ins and outs of publishing and the role they can play in successfully marketing and promoting their book. I'm going to recommend P.J.'s book to every author and editor I work with."
—Sandy Siegle, Media and Sales Director, Timber Press

So many people have supported my writing over the years; please accept my gratitude for your constant and consistent support. A special "thank you" goes out to my niece, Kelly, and nephew, Rick; my son, Roy (hugs and kisses); my sisters, Ann and Claudia; my brother-in-law, Dick; my girlfriends, Deanna, Karen, Carol, and Billie; my life companion, Matthew; computer wizard, Matt; colleague, Aditi; writing teacher, Nancy; and photographer, Michael.

If you are interested in hands-on book success guidance, join me at theartandbusinessofwriting.com conference or contact me at pjcampbellwriter.com.

P.J. Campbell

1 | What Happens After the Manuscript is Delivered to the Publisher?

Congratulations, you have succeeded in getting your book published! The odds of having a book published by a traditional publisher are slim, to say the least. Even though there are over 275,000 books published in the United States annually, an even greater number of book submissions are rejected. You can walk into any publisher's or editor's office and not be able to see his or her desk (and sometimes even the floor) under the overwhelming towers of manuscripts. This doesn't even take into account the number of online submissions.

Writing a book may be the most significant feat of your entire life. You've just joined the ranks with those following one of the most sought-after claim-to-fame paths. You've chosen to put yourself out into the public eye and open the vault to your inner depository of knowledge and creativity for all to draw upon. This is by no means an easy task and yet, here you are—you've done it! So, give yourself a BIG pat on the back.

However, just when you thought you were going to sit back and take a breather, that's unfortunately not going to happen. You thought it was tough delivering your manuscript on time, but the next step in selling your book is getting the word out. There is a considerable difference between the processes of submitting and eventually delivering your book to the publisher and promoting it in order to produce the projected sales. The key difference is the time line. Yes, you were under the editor's gun to deliver your manuscript on time, but if you needed to buy a few weeks or months, it's quite possible that you were permitted some leeway. When it comes to selling your book to readers, you will not have the luxury of extending the amount of time you have to prove yourself—the public, the bookseller, and the media will not be so forgiving. You have approximately six-to-eight weeks from the time your book is available in the bookstores to demonstrate that your book is indispensable. The bookstore's real estate (shelf and table space) carries a very high ticket price, and if your book does not produce as predicted, it will quickly lose favor and be forgotten.

2 | What Can the Author do to Generate Publicity, Promotion, and Sales?

Whether this is your first book or your tenth, every book needs particular attention from the author. The author's participation in the publicity, promotion, and sale of his or her book can make the difference between winning and losing at the bookselling game. In fact, unless you're a celebrity or have a built-in audience (following), it's ultimately up to you to generate the majority of book sales.

An author with a "platform" has the ability to reach out and touch an enormous number of potential book buyers. A platform refers to what the author can bring to the table. This includes your credentials, website, email list, blog, community relationships, professional degrees, and memberships or officer standings in organizations or associations. Your platform also consists of past and pending speaking engagements, publicity contacts, sponsors, corporate tie-ins, and buy-backs (these are the books that the author agrees to purchase to either resell or give away in conjunction with the book campaign). All of these resources will help drive book sales and illustrate to readers that you are an authority (I find it interesting that this word begins with "author") whom they can trust.

Deciding how to maximize your time in support of your book campaign will require careful analysis of what you, as the author, are capable of in terms of producing book sales. Take an inventory of your resources and leave nothing for chance, as the journey you're about to take will demand your constant, disciplined focus.

3 | Booking Publicity

Publicity is by far the most important aspect of your overall book campaign. (If your publisher is handling your publicity, then you may not need to do all that is suggested in this section; however, I strongly encourage you to work in tandem with the publisher.) Creating a powerful, eye-catching press release and press kit is a priority (more information on how to do this in the "Publicity" chapter).

Generate a list of personal media contacts, including national and local television, radio, and print outlets to which you can announce the release of your new book. If you have previously appeared on television or radio or have been interviewed by magazines or newspapers, then these media contacts may be interested in talking to you about your new book. Typically, it is easier to secure an interview or appearance if you already have relationships with individuals in the media, as you are already known to them. These people are familiar with you and know how well you interview, which elevates their comfort level and makes them more likely to work with you again.

If you have previous interviews or appearances recorded on DVD or some other format, these can be utilized to gain additional media support. Generally, network television stations want to see footage of an author prior to committing to having him or her appear on one of their programs. You can also upload your recordings to YouTube, where they will be easily accessible for the media. The easier you make it for the press to view your media history, the better your chances are for a repeat engagement. You should also offer to send media contacts complimentary copies of your book and press release. Be sure to include a time frame during which you'll be available for an interview in their area.

If you're unfamiliar with a place's local media, visit easymedialist.com. If you have no media contacts or have never been interviewed before but have friends or family members with connections, ask them to intercede on your behalf—personal recommendations can open press room doors.

4 | The Author's Sales and Promotion Efforts

What can authors do to generate sales and promotion for themselves? Bookstore appearances are commonly used to achieve this; however, unless you're a known celebrity in your field or in general, you can probably expect a low turnout. There are some less-typical "speak and sign" events that can prove successful.

People who are interested and engaged are more likely to purchase a book. Can you offer a class, demonstration, or consultation of some kind in conjunction with your bookstore appearance? For example, if you authored a craft book, you could give a class or even a series of classes centered around your book about sewing, knitting, beading, et cetera. The book could be the ticket price for the attendees. Or, maybe you're an expert cake decorator and your book gives instructions for making specialty holiday cakes. Try to put on a baking class at a local bakery and have a bookstore sell the tickets (this, of course, guarantees that your book will be sold to the number of attendees). If your book is highly specialized in this way, try raffling off free consultations to be scheduled after your event.

Also, do you have any giveaway items for your book? Imagine that you've written a book about being organized. You could provide free pens, sticky notes, or notebooks all branded with your book's title. Providing refreshments is also a good idea—free food always encourages people to attend an event.

What about circulating fliers around your hometown and nearby universities and libraries? The flier should contain a brief overview of your book, the ISBN, the publisher, your web address, and where the book can be purchased. These promotional fliers can be distributed in conjunction with a bookstore appearance or act as "stand-alone" advertisements.

5 | Author Sponsorships, Corporate Tie-Ins, and Products

Some authors have sponsors for their book. This could be a food company for a culinary author, a credit card company for a motivational and self-improvement author, a sporting goods manufacturer for a sports author, or a cosmetics company for a beauty or fashion author—the list of potential sponsorships for authors is limitless. Here are some ways that sponsorships can be beneficial:

- Sponsors can offer exposure for your book on their product packaging.
- An author could be a spokesperson for a product that will include his or her book on the packaging or will include redeemable coupons for the book.
- Sponsors can include notices about your book in customers' billing statements.
- Some sponsors cover touring expenses in exchange for your promotion of their product.

Also, corporations may purchase your book in bulk (hundreds or thousands of books) to give to their clients or employees. This is often the case when an author is an employee who has written a book that has some connection to his or her employer or the company's product. Establishing your own product tie-in can also be a great springboard for your book. For example, Julie Pech, "The Chocolate Therapist" (thechocolatetherapist.com), has developed her own line of chocolate; in fact, she even bought a chocolate factory. In addition to actually making chocolate, Julie wrote *The Chocolate Therapist* and is currently working on another book about pairing chocolate and wine. Because of her product, she has a built-in audience and following. She speaks all over the world, selling chocolate and books. If you are a consultant or provide some other service to clients, then you could sell your book to them so that they have a handy reference for your services.

6 | The Author's Online Support Efforts

Offering signed copies of your book at no extra charge on your website is another way to accumulate email addresses and sell copies of your book to a targeted audience. Also, join Amazon Connect: Author Blogs, a program that gives authors direct access to their readers. Authors can generate messages and post them to the Amazon.com home pages, which are seen by all Amazon book-buying customers. The posted messages will also appear on the author's title page and profile page. All of this will increase your exposure on the largest book retailer in the world.

To find out more, visit amazon.com/gp/arms/role/learn-more.html and go to the "For the Community" section.

There are also myriad social media outlets that are worth joining, such as Facebook, You Tube, LinkedIn, Flickr, Twitter, and MySpace. Also, creating your own website and blog will support sales and provide a place to direct your readers for more information about you and your book. This kind of web space will give you exposure and allow you to accumulate contacts, and blogging on pertinent sites and linking back to your website and blog will add value to your author profile while supporting book sales. With SEO keyword density, a blog can do volumes in terms of spreading the buzz about your book. For more in-depth information, see the "Online Promotion" chapter.

You can also create an account with author.filedby.com. This is one of the best websites created specifically to highlight all authors with a free page listing, which includes your bio, book, links to booksellers, and more. They also offer two other page-listing packages that cost $99 or $399. Filedby has gained a tremendous amount of media attention and publishers are advising their authors to sign up.

Joining an online bookseller affiliate program for a bookstore is another proactive and free way to promote your book, generate sales, and receive a commission for referrals from your website when books are sold. Look into the affiliate programs provided by some of the following booksellers and query your local bookstore, writers association, and other book or author-related websites:

- amazon.com
- barnesandnoble.com
- news.bookweb.org/news/6229

Email blasts are a way to target specific groups of people about your book. Sending an email blast on your own might seem simple, and it is if you only have a few names, but if you want to strike a wider audience, you may need to enlist an email provider. Check with your Internet Service Provider (ISP) and research the Internet.

7 | Webinars, Teleseminars, and Podcasts

Webinars, teleseminars, and podcasts are popular ways of reaching targeted audiences without leaving your home or office. Many organizations, corporations, and associations host webinars nationally and internationally. The overarching benefit to these digital media is the ability to appear in front of an unlimited number of attendees all across the globe with ease. Often, the book is included in the ticket price, which guarantees that a certain number of copies will be sold. The book can also be sold by booksellers as an add-on to the event.

Teleseminars can be as effective as webinars when Power Point presentations or other on-screen visual support accompanies the audio presentation. Attendees can phone in from their offices while viewing their computer screens, or can choose to limit their participation to just the audio portion of the program. Listeners can also phone in or send email questions to the speaker or host. In some ways, teleseminars are better attended because participants are not required to be in front of a computer and can receive the visual support after the event if desired. Your book can be offered to attendees in the same manner as with webinars.

While podcasts are one-way presentations, they can still be very effective in selling your book. Your audio or visual presentations can be downloaded to your website and made available to the public. The public can then access the podcast at no charge, or you can ask for a fee. You could offer a brief teaser segment for free and then link them to a bookseller.

8 | An Educated Author Is Empowered

There is no substitute for being a great writer, but an even better writer is one who is informed about the goings-on in the writer's world.

Subscribe to writers' magazines to stay abreast of trends in the publishing industry. These magazines sponsor writers' contests that are, unlike many writing contests, legitimate. There are a number of authors who, upon winning or placing in the top ten contestants, land publishing contracts, are noticed by agents, and/or are asked to contribute to the sponsoring magazines. It is possible that a writer who has won a writing contest will command attention from other sources, including local television stations, newspapers, radio stations, or magazines. Winning writers may also be invited to speak at local libraries, high schools, universities, chambers of commerce, and more.

Some of the best writers' publications include *Writers Digest* (writersdigest.com), *The Writers Journal* (writersjournal.com), *The Writer* (writermag.com), *Poets & Writers* (pw.org), and *The Writer's Chronicle* (awpwriter.org/magazine).

Join writers' groups, organizations, chats, and societies. Writers' groups will enable you to share your writing with your peers and receive valuable feedback. You will also enhance your skills by listening to what other writers are working on and by considering their comments. These groups are a safe place to present unfinished, rough drafts of your work. Membership in these groups opens the door to their members lists, newsletters, discussion boards, and chats. What better way to increase your publishing comprehension and writing ability than to harmonize with industry experts? Here is a list of resources for finding writers' groups, workshops, and conventions:

- keepwriting.com/allwriters/wgroups.htm
- writersconf.org
- awpwriter.org
- writers.net/resources/resources_chats.php
- writerschatroom.com
- scbwi.org
- womenswritersnsw.org
- writing.shawguides.com
- writersdigest.com/conferencescene
- writersonlineworkshops.com

If you are not able to join a formalized writers' gathering, establish your own by connecting with writers in your local community by contacting your local libraries and bookstores and posting fliers.

Attending writing classes can also be beneficial. Here are a few websites that are worth checking out:

- writersdigest.com
- writingclasses.com
- mediabistro.com/courses

9 | Saturation in the Marketplace

Is it possible to over-promote your book? You can never have too much of a good thing, right?

The answer is, you cannot get enough publicity for your book. Whether you appear on Oprah, or your book is reviewed in *The New York Times*, or you broadcast your own radio show, there is no such thing as too much publicity. Even so-called "bad" publicity is good, to a degree.

Promotion through advertisements in magazines and newspapers and on radio and television stations, billboards, and the Internet is good if you have the budget to repeat the ads. If you don't, then you might be disappointed with the results. You cannot overdo advertising in a way that will adversely affect the sale of your book. In the case of promotion, more is better.

Public appearance is a great means of receiving word-of-mouth promotional support; however, pay attention to the logistical proximity, demographics of potential attendees, and timing. It's a good idea to book events that are spaced apart physically (about thirty minutes of drive time between each is a good rule). Consider the characteristics of the guests. If you're hitting similar audiences, you might inadvertently diminish the attendance at some of your events. For this reason, scheduling back-to-back appearances in the same community can be disastrous.

Many bookstores and organizations will either ask to be first on the list of events or demand that they host the only event within a certain mile radius. Public appearance is the only arm of the promotional process that will suffer if you over-saturate the same markets. If you must choose one community to saturate, do so systematically by selecting different days of the week. This will allow you to attain a more varied audience.

10 | Create Promotion Offline and Hands-On

You should have a business card that reflects your published title(s) (unless you have way too many to list). Every time you meet someone and pass along your business card, you are, in effect, promoting your work.

Passing out fliers at local shops will cost a few dollars, and if one person buys your book as a result, then the cost is worth it. Fliers also help to generate word-of-mouth promotion. Someone who picks up a flier could tell some of his or her friends, which will result in more books sold. Word-of-mouth is a powerful and consistent method of selling any product, including your book.

Local movie theaters might be receptive to handing out bookmarks or postcards if they're playing a movie that relates to your book. In return, you can post comments on their website and your own about the movie.

You can also offer your book on consignment to local merchants that are in some way connected to the subject matter of your book. For example, a book about the environment and sustainability might be relevant to many businesses in your area as the "green" movement gains popularity. With consignment, no money trades hands until the merchant sells your book. In exchange for their willingness to give some of their shop's space to your book, you could offer to blog about their store, send an email blast about the shop, or create a link on your website to the store's website. Everyone enjoys free advertising and promotion.

Local bookstores and libraries support local authors and will welcome fliers, bookmarks, postcards, and other promotional materials that they can offer to their customers. These are just a few inexpensive ways to consider supporting your book's release that are more hands-on than online.

11 | The Author's Bio, Photograph, and Endorsements

Your biographical details provide more information for the book jacket and allow your readers to get to know you. Don't be concerned about giving the editor too much background—he or she will know what to keep and what to discard.

Providing an updated headshot photo for your book's press release and/or book jacket is one more thing that you can do to help the publisher gather all of the necessary elements of your book's package. If you don't have a good picture, have one taken by a friend or professional. Your picture will also be needed for publicity; readers like to see the author, as it gives them a sense of who you are.

Endorsements are powerful. They act as "social proof" that you are who you say you are and that your book has "the goods." Praise separates you from other authors. Think about it: Considering the number of books being published, why would someone who doesn't know who you are pick up your book when it's sitting right next to another one about a similar topic? Endorsements command attention from book buyers, readers, and the media. Public approval from endorsers is a way that an author can flex his or her muscles.

Gathering endorsements can be iffy and somewhat uncomfortable, but if you start by thanking your potential endorser, then you might just be received with open arms. Start by asking friends, associates, or colleagues who possess the authority to write statements that will encourage readers to select your book. Don't be afraid to send your endorsement request to television personalities, celebrities, or anyone with whom you think the topic would resonate—you might just get lucky.

12 | Author Questionnaire

Many publishers will ask an author to complete an Author Questionnaire, which is a way for the publisher's team of support people to get to know you. In the end, it will save you time in conveying all of the assorted details requested and needed by your publisher.

Here's a sampling of what to expect on the AQ form:

- Personal information: Name, title of book, home address and phone number, business address and phone, email address, and fax number.

- Professional information: Your day job and position, college education, professional honors or awards, and association or organization memberships

- Other books you've had published: Title, publisher, pub date, sales history, foreign publications, book club selection, and any applicable coauthor information

- Are you a contributor to a regular column or other media outlet? If so, name the publications or media sources.

- Do you have an existing speaking schedule? Give detailed information, including the hosting venue, location, dates, and reason for your appearance.
- Whatever you have done in the past and whatever you are planning to do in the future, up to, during, and after the release of your book where it concerns your book must be conveyed to the editor. Some examples: media appearances, speaking engagements, sponsorships, affiliations, awards, travel plans, availability, et cetera.

→

13 | The Best Way to Interact with Your Publisher

"A cooperative and friendly nature will sustain your publishing relationship." This pretty much says it all.

Now that your book has been published, how do you ensure that your publisher listens to your needs, answers your questions, and fulfills their contractual obligations?

The term "publisher" actually has several different meanings. The publisher or publishing company is the "company" that will produce your book. Your book will carry its imprint and will be sold by its sales force. The "publisher" also refers to the publishing team as a whole, which includes the publisher, editor, marketer, publicist, events coordinator, creative service designer, sales reps, and distribution center.

There's also a "publisher" position within the publishing house. The publisher is the manager over a particular product line, category, or genre who supervises the editors. He or she is responsible for overseeing the business of publishing the titles within his or her domain. This business involves allocation of funds, determining the print run, projection of sales and revenue (ROI), and distribution of sales through the sales channels (bookstores, mass market, specialty stores, online, wholesalers, and other outlets).

Once your book approaches the official "on-sale" date, other publishing team members will begin to contact you. The timing of their interaction with you can vary according to your book's content, but generally, you will hear from the publicity, marketing, and events teams approximately three-to-six months ahead of your book's debut in the marketplace. Working in tandem with these departments in an amicable manner will go far to enhance the support you receive. The more you can offer to help, the more you increase their attention; however, be sensitive to their direction. If they want your input, they will ask for it.

Meeting with the rest of the publisher's sales support departments on a need-to basis (determined by you and them) will take the mystery out of what's happening with your book and keep everyone informed as to your book's progress.

14 | Building Rapport with Your Publishing Partners

The editor will be your partner throughout the entire publishing process. He or she will speak on your behalf to the rest of the publishing team, who will facilitate the sale of your book through their respective modes of operation.

At the beginning of the publishing process, your editor is your chief contact for all questions and concerns. Because his or her income is based, in part, on the sales of the product line in which your book is positioned, he or she is the one with the greatest stake in the success of your book. (The product line refers to the category under which your title will fall for book retailers. For example, if you're looking for a mystery book in a bookstore, you will find it in the section labeled, "Mystery." Classifying titles makes it easier for readers to locate books and assists the booksellers in shelving them.)

Developing a friendly, but not overly familiar relationship with your editor will make all the difference in the quality and quantity of attention you receive in terms of having your needs met. The editor is your publisher's in-house advocate for your title and should do whatever he or she can to influence the publisher's backing from every department, including sales, creative, marketing, publicity, printing, and distribution.

It's helpful to establish a check-in process with your editor, such as agreeing to meet over the phone for a few minutes biweekly or monthly to check the progress of the book campaign. Developing a solid relationship with your editor from the first point of contact is, relative to the publishing process, as important as breathing. Your editor is your greatest ally and will go to battle for you if necessary. Consider him or her the captain of your publishing team.

At the appropriate point during the publishing process, you will be introduced to the rest of the players who will influence and drive the sale of your book. Whether you align with your marketer, publicist, events coordinator, or production designer, the book's campaign strategy will still be led by your editor and your publisher. In your dealings with the other members of the publishing team, treat them as you would your editor: be respectful, polite, and above all, be forthcoming about your support capabilities. The worst thing you can do is over-promise and under-deliver. If you agree to contact your media acquaintances and it eventually turns out that you have very few (or none at all), you're sending a message of untrustworthiness to the entire team. As is the case with anything, it's much harder to fix a mistake than to do something correctly in the beginning. Your honesty will pay off in the end.

15 | Author Contacts

Marketing, publicity, and events staff will be curious to know who you know and what you've done in the past in terms of your book or previously published books. They will be interested in any contacts you have including members of the media, sponsors, organizations, corporations, and associations, and will most likely want to use these people or organizations to support the sale of your book. Providing an in-depth account of these resources will give them a foundation on which to build their campaign and drive sales. Much of this information will be asked of you in the Author Questionnaire (AQ); however, you might have new contacts or have forgotten a few since you provided your publisher with that document.

It is also possible that more contacts and details can be discovered through conversations and brainstorms with the publisher, since you, the author, might not have realized that those contacts or details were important. Expose all details to your publishing team, because you never know what might catch their attention and create excitement. All of this information helps make up your platform.

Here are a couple of general tips on interacting with your publishing team:

- Make yourself as available as possible to your publishing team. They will be as respectful of your time as you are of theirs.

- Emphasize the potential for mutual benefit and approach the relationship and project as a collaboration. This will sustain your relationship with the entire team and may result in future publishing opportunities.
- Honesty and charisma can work wonders in terms of sales support for you and your title.

16 | What Can the Author Expect from the Editor?

Before final negotiations with your editor, you should have a general idea of how they intend to design, create, promote, publicize, and sell your book. Once you've signed the contract with your publisher, your editor will develop the book's campaign (the publisher's plans for your book) in detail.

The editor will want to know what you, the author, can do to reinforce this campaign and bolster sales of your book. You may be asked to complete an Author Questionnaire (AQ), a detailed document in which an author lists his or her contacts including media, corporations, associations, sponsors, and endorsements, and other related experiences, such as speaking engagements, presentations, op-eds, essays, and articles.

Depending on the publisher, the editor may or may not assist you with the development of the text for the book. Their copyeditors will proceed with a line edit (literally going through the text line-by-line) in order to ensure that the text is grammatically and mechanically correct and free of spelling errors and repetition—essentially, they make sure that the book flows systematically. Your book, whether it be fiction or non-fiction, may be vetted to make sure that the content is factually correct. Vetting is more likely to take place with nonfiction titles; however, when fiction includes real places, persons, and events, it must also be checked for accuracy.

17 | Support from Creative Services

Creative Services, or, the publisher's art department, collaborates with the publisher, editor, and marketer to create and design your book's jacket (front and back cover) and interior layout. They will select the paper stock and typefaces and may work with designers or photographers to create the cover and back images. The entirety of the book—front cover, back cover, and each interior page—is handled by the design team. You may or may not have input into your book's final visual concept.

If you disagree with the cover choice, typeface, layout, or any aspect of the book product, let your editor know. He or she will take your concerns into consideration and decide whether or not your suggestions should be addressed by the design team. If the editor or designer doesn't make the changes you suggested, state your objections to your editor once more, and then drop it. Ultimately, the publishing team's experience will overshadow what you have to say and your publisher will produce the book in a way that they believe will achieve their sales goals.

The Sales Department will also have a say in the cover of the book as they receive feedback from retail book buyers. Sometimes, buyers from national book chains can dramatically influence a book's design. Most publishers respect and value the judgment of national bookstore chains (such as Borders and Barnes & Noble), as they are an authority on what sells and are likely to sell the largest number of your books. Even Amazon, while not a brick and mortar bookstore, is included in this category, as it's the number one online bookseller. It is not unusual for a book jacket to be changed at the request of Amazon buyers in order to improve online appearance.

Working closely with the editor and marketer, the "packaging" of the book is the Creative Services Department's primary focus. They develop, along with the bindery (or, printer), the book's production schedule. Creative Services is also responsible for co-creating the publisher's seasonal catalogs, which will feature your book among the publisher's other titles. Depending on the publisher, they will follow either a two or three-season calendar, which are broken up as follows: Fall/Winter, Spring/Summer (in the case of a two-season calendar) and Fall, Winter, Spring/Summer (in the case of a three-season calendar). These catalogs announce the publication of your book to booksellers, libraries, media outlets, wholesale distributors, corporate clients, and other retail outlets. They are distributed at publishing industry trade shows including Book Expo of America, North Atlantic Independent Booksellers Association, Pacific Northwest Booksellers Association, and others. Today, it is common for publishers to offer an electronic version, partly for convenience and partly to be "green."

$\rightarrow$

18 | Support from the Marketing Team

A marketer acts as the "air traffic controller," if you will, bringing together all of the components of your book campaign. They are responsible for developing the overall promotional strategy for your book. Working in conjunction with the other departments that will champion your book, including editorial, creative, publicity, events, sales, distribution, and production, the marketing team is the driving force behind your book and has the power to make or break it. They are responsible for the budget allocation per-title and determine where the money will be spent in order to promote your book. In some publishing houses, however, some or all of the marketing tasks fall to the editor, rather than the marketer, so find out who in your publishing house will take the helm for your book. In the end, this individual may have more power than anyone else on your publisher's team.

Marketing determines the process by which your title will go to the bookselling marketplace. The marketer's job encompasses or overlaps with almost every aspect of the publishing process, from assisting in the publishing schedule, creating collateral materials (such as fliers, postcards, email blasts, advertisements, et cetera), to meeting with the author, agent, and in-house associates to collaborate for the good of the title.

Marketers also work closely with the publicity and events departments to determine which media outlets and venues to target. Your marketer may decide that your book deserves national attention and consider outlets such as long-lead magazines (*Atlantic Monthly*, *Vogue*, et cetera), national television networks (ABC,

NBC, CBS), national radio (NPR), or national newspapers (*The New York Times, The Wall Street Journal, USA Today*). He or she might decide instead that local media is more appropriate for your book. Listed below are some common local media outlets and resources for locating and contacting the ones near you:

- Local television stations: newslink.org/stattele.html
- Local radio stations: dir.yahoo.com/News_and_Media/Radio/Programs
- Local newspapers: onlinenewspapers.com/usstate/usatable.htm
- Local magazines: bookmarket.com/regmags.htm

Marketers will also consider what you personally can do to promote your book. Here are some questions that you might be presented with when collaborating on a marketing strategy:

- Will you be a good spokesperson for your book?
- Do you need media training?
- As the author, are you available for media appointments, or is there someone else the media should speak to about your book?
- Are you a good public speaker?
- Have you ever done a live presentation in front of an audience?
- Do your speaking skills need to be polished?
- Have you taken advantage of any of the social media outlets, including Facebook, MySpace, or Twitter?

Developing a book campaign strategy is a priority and must be approached systematically. You can reach your goals if you have a plan and take notice of what's working and change what's not. The collaborative effort of all parties, including the author, is essential.

19 | Support from the Publicity Team

Major publishing houses have an in-house publicity department. The publicist's responsibility is to execute the publicity plans for the book as put forth by the publicity and marketing teams. He or she will be your press contact and will schedule appointments for you to meet with the media, write press releases, and send out review copies. These copies, also known as galleys, are un-edited, not-for-sale copies of the book. Not all books have galleys, as they are an expense that many publishers don't incorporate into the title's campaign strategy. They may produce bound manuscripts or blads (book layout and design) instead. Whatever promotional materials are created for your book are included by the publicist in his or her press kit distribution. Your publicist will also begin pitching your book to the appropriate long-lead magazines (if this is part of the plan) six months before the publication date, which is generally two-to-four weeks after the ship date.

The publicist also updates everyone within the sales support team on the status of your book's media attention. Having access to up-to-the-minute press bookings is essential for the sales department, since they are pitching your book to their customers. Media hits can influence the "buy" of any bookselling outlet.

The bottom line with publicity is that you need it in order to earn your title mass appeal. Therefore, whether or not your publisher provides a publicist, you must figure out a way to gain media coverage. Something to keep in mind is that the in-house publicist who is working on your book is also working on a number of other titles simultaneously and may not be able to give your book adequate attention. Ask your editor for a list of media outlets to which your book has been pitched. The publicist usually will not provide you with a list of their contacts' names, but they should provide you with a general list of outlets that they've contacted on behalf of your book.

If you feel that your book is not getting enough publicity, due either to lack of effort by the publicist or for other reasons, you may want to look into hiring your own publicist, who will be able to devote more time and effort to your book alone.

20 | Support from the Sales Department

The sales force is responsible for presenting and selling your book to retail outlets, including brick and mortar stores, online stores, specialty stores, and libraries. Many publishers also have a corporate sales department that sells your book in quantity to companies for the purposes of training and development or for employee and customer gifts. Additionally, a wholesale sales division sells to wholesale distributors who, in turn, resell the book to retail outlets that might be unable to purchase the book according to the publisher's terms. Many independent bookstores purchase books though wholesalers (such as Baker & Taylor).

Sales representatives present titles to their book buyers about four-to-six months prior to your book's release. This gives the bookseller time to consider all of the books being released by various publishers. The book buyer will ultimately put their dollars where they feel they are likely to reap the best return on their investment.

With the help of feedback from the sales department, the publisher can more easily determine the print run of a given title, thereby avoiding over- or under-producing your book. Publishers hold weekly, biweekly, monthly, or seasonal sales and marketing meetings in order to support the sales team in their efforts. At these meetings, updated information regarding media, events, and implementation of marketing plans and funds is shared with the group.

Most publishers place most of their attention on their front list (newest books released), but also continue to push the sale of the books on the back list (those published six months or more past their pub date) that have a proven track record for continued sales. The back list is the bread and butter of any publishing house.

21 | Will the Publisher Schedule Events?

Appearing in front of live audiences and conducting presentations via the web (teleseminars, webinars, podcasts, or online chats) are ways in which an author can support the sale of his or her book by speaking to book and author enthusiasts.

Some publishers incorporate events into the publicity or sales departments, while others have a separate events department dedicated to arranging speaking engagements and other supporting events for their authors. Find out how your publisher is set up to handle your speaking schedule.

Many venues will permit the author to have his or her book for sale in conjunction with the appearance. The publisher's events contact will find out if the venue has a preferred method for handling book sales. Below is a list of options they will propose to venues other than bookstores:

- Arrange for a bookstore to come on-site to the venue to sell copies of the book.
- Ask the venue to purchase the book and include the book in their ticket price.
- Have the venue purchase the book and sell it in the back of the room.
- The author can purchase books and sell for him or herself.

Venues that the publisher's events department may consider for speaking engagements include conferences and conventions, local bookstores, libraries, charity associations, press clubs, resorts, and more.

One of the keys to booking an event is timing. Allow at least three months lead time in scheduling, as all venues need time to promote your appearance and prepare (additional details can be found in the "Events" chapter).

22 | Licensing and Rights Department

Did you ever wonder how a magazine, website, newspaper, or any other information source was allowed to include a portion of a published book's text? Within the publishing house, there are departments that handle the sale and use of the book's content in various forms.

First, there is the Licensing Department, which is in the business of permitting the use of portions of a book's content in alignment with the contractual terms agreed upon by the publisher and the purchaser of the content.

Second, the Sub-Rights Department is in charge of licensing or selling portions of the book's content or the entire book to another party, who is then permitted to sell it to clients.

These departments are also in control of selling translation rights, which grant permission to reprint the book in a foreign language. Additionally, any use of the book's content through any and all electronic media, such as websites, iPod/iPhone applications, audio recordings, and any other downloadable formats are all handled by the Sub-Rights and Licensing Departments.

Passages, chapters, or any other sound bytes (small portions of the book's text) must be licensed before use. Normally, there is a fee for that usage which varies according to intended use; however, this same content can be used for advertising or marketing purposes without a fee. The percentage of revenue from licensing is subject to the publisher's contract.

Below, take a closer look at the range of rights and licensing opportunities for a book. These outlets can add more value to your book and produce extra royalties for you.

Types of Licensing:

- English, non-English Licensing: Gives consent to publish a book in the English language in areas outside of the United States or Canada, including locations in which English is the spoken language.
- Translation Rights: Authorizes a foreign language publisher to publish the book in their native language.

- Paperback Reproduction: Gives permission to the buyer to recreate a hardcover book in paperback format for distribution to a mass market or trade paperback publisher. (Mass market books are the smaller-trim sized books that are commonly found in grocery stores, discount chains, and airports. Trade paperbacks are traditionally the same size as hardcover books but have paper front and back covers.)

- Hardcover Reprint: The right to republish an out of print title in a hardcover reprint version, or to produce a custom hardcover publication with the original publisher. (An out of print book is a book that the publisher no longer carries in its inventory.)

- Large Print Edition: Permits the publisher to enlarge the book's text.

- Audio Rights: Grants the buyer the audio recording of a book's content, either in full or abridged.

- Electronic Outlets: Gives the purchaser the authority to reproduce a book's content in any and/or all available electronic media.

- Merchandising: Allows the buyer to use a book's text for calendars, cards, puzzles, and other gift-related, paper-constructed items.

The ways in which your book's content will be used will depend upon your author-publisher contract. Some publishers may refer to some of the above usages in different terms, so check your contract and confer with your editor if you have any questions about the re-purposing of your book's content.

23 | The Publisher's Distribution Center

The DC is the publisher's warehouse. It's where the bindery ships the book when production is complete. It is vital that the book be released into the marketplace in accordance with the specific publication time frame, as every component of the book's campaign depends on it. Imagine, for a moment, that you and the publisher's team have been working for months on the release of your book into the marketplace. Your publicity is beginning, you have a full speaking schedule, email blasts are going out, local advertising has been placed, but there are no books in the bookstores or online! What do you think this would do to your book's projected sales results? You guessed it—the sales would not even come close to meeting yours or your publisher's expectations.

The marketer and editor work closely with the warehouse to ensure the timely release of the book. The sales department is also in regular contact with them for the purposes of expediting their customers' purchase orders.

Inquire as to the location of your publisher's DC. This is good information to have when estimating the delivery time of your book to a bookstore or speaking venue.

→

24 | E-Book and Audio Book Formats

Assuming that there is a demand for your book's content, subject matter, or genre, the publisher may decide to convert your book to an e-format and/or into an audio book, but understand that there is an expense to the publisher for this conversion. As we move forward in the age of technology and as "going green" gains mainstream popularity, more books will be available electronically.

While it may be advantageous to have an e-book, the downside of it is the loss of control of the content. In the music industry, we have witnessed how the unauthorized duplication of an artist's music has become a monster to deal with. Unfortunately, making a book available electronically can create a similar situation.

Audio books sell well and appeal to those who have a limited amount of time to casually absorb a book by reading it. Audio versions offer readers a way to listen while commuting, lounging, working, et cetera. Audio books are also welcomed and well-utilized by the visually impaired.

An important question to ask is whether or not the royalties for the audio version of your book will be equal to those for your hard copy. It is likely to be less, but discuss this with your editor, as it will follow the terms of your contract.

25 | Publisher's Pace

In terms of pacing, the publishing industry is at best a steady, but usually slow business. Printed books have been around for hundreds of years and have certainly caught up with the digital age, but the actual publishing process, that is, the act of getting a book to press, can take up to two years. One of the main reasons for the delay in publishing a book is the sheer volume of submissions. Acquisition editors receive an estimated 2.6 million proposals annually. Additionally, the actual editing of a manuscript, in many cases, is outsourced, which adds to the length of time it takes for a book to come together.

Once a book has been contracted, the length of time that it takes for it to move from manuscript to a finished, bound book can take eighteen months or more. What's going on at your publishing house during this time? The actual printing of a book may only take a few months; in fact, depending on the printer's location, this process can be turned around even more quickly than that. The editor is working on cleaning up the manuscript so that it's in perfect order while the design team is creating several versions of the book's layout and front and back cover design. The marketing department is collaborating with editorial for the final title and other book product components and with sales to ensure that the predicted print run will be sold. Publicity and events are pitching the book to media outlets in hopes of further underscoring the sales predictions. Needless to say, all of this takes a very long time to orchestrate and execute. Also, don't forget that yours is not your publisher's only book.

The best way to speed up your book's publication is to land a high-profile, national media event (such as an appearance on Oprah), but keep in mind that even this does not guarantee that your book will be published more quickly. Publicity is short-lived and publishers look for press opportunities to link the book to headlines. If you don't have any imminent press attention that can influence the sale of your book, then be patient—it's worth the wait.

26 | Publicity Budget

Before you think about putting your own money into promoting your book, consider the projected publication quantity (the number of books the publisher is printing). Does your publisher expect to sell 5,000 or 50,000 copies? While your overall budget should not be based on the number of books the publisher is printing, the print run can provide a clue as to how the publisher will support your book with their internal and/or external resources.

If the production run for your book is lower than 8,000-10,000 copies, this might be an indication that your book is viewed as small-to-medium-sized relative to the publisher's entire list of titles. If you find your book in this position, have a frank conversation with your editor about the publisher's plans for promoting and backing your title. Keep in mind that your book's position can vary based on the size of the publishing house. For example, at Random House or Simon & Schuster, a small print run like the one discussed would indicate a "C-level" book; however, at a smaller, independent publisher such as Newmarket Press, Overlook Press, or Sourcebooks, Inc. (bookmarket.com/101publishers. htm), or at an imprint of one of the larger publishers, including Knopf, Pocketbooks, or Scribner, a small print run can command a sufficient, in-house, financially-supported book plan.

Thinking realistically will help you to decide if it's worthwhile for you to ante up some of your own money to support your book. Before you do anything, discuss with your publisher how they intend to publicize and financially support your book.

No one has more to gain from a book's success than the author. Investing a reasonable amount of money into the publicity, promotion, and sale of your book will affect the book's overall campaign and will be money well spent.

27 | Allocating Your Budget Dollars for Publicity

Generating publicity is by far the best thing you can do to promote awareness and the sale of your book. The principal percentage (50-75%) of your budget's first allocation should go to a public relations firm or freelance publicist who specializes in your book's topic or genre.

A PR firm or publicist will cost anywhere from $1,000 to $50,000, depending on the length of time you wish to engage their services and publicity plans. If your title is one that will need constant publicity, then it might be more cost effective to contract a public relations firm on a retainer's fee. This is also the case if your book is what is referred to as an "evergreen" title, meaning that, the longer it sits on the bookstores' shelves, it will gain, rather than lose, momentum.

Publicists' fees take into account their time spent on creating press releases and press kits and pitching your book to the media via the phone, email, fax, snail mail, or in person. Outside publicists or PR firms work in tandem with your publisher, reporting their progress regarding media response and bookings to both you and your publisher.

In the book publishing world, the advantages of hiring publicity experts make them well worth their fees. Selecting the right publicist or PR firm for your book is critical. If you decide to hire your own publicist, make sure to notify your publisher in order to avoid duplicating their in-house publicity efforts. Also, remember that there are no guarantees when it comes to generating publicity; anyone who makes promises about what they can achieve is leading you down the garden path.

28 | Should I Hire My Own PR Agent?

Hiring a publicist to focus on your title can significantly increase the exposure of your book to the media. Even though the publisher will provide some publicity support for your book, keep in mind that the in-house publicist is also responsible for other titles, which cuts into the amount of time devoted to your title.

There are a number of incentives to hire your own publicist, including:

- Contracting an outside publicist will ensure increased attention for your book.
- You will be able to access the publicist directly.
- You can more easily dictate the course of action you want the publicist to follow.
- The publicist will be answerable to the terms and goals for your book's publicity that you have both agreed upon contractually.

- The PR firm might have connections that the publisher does not.
- You can establish the length of time that you want the publicist to work on your book. As long as you are willing to pay, he or she will keep pitching, provided it makes sense and produces the desired results.
- You may be traveling and wish to tie in publicity in the marketplace but don't have the time to arrange interviews.

In a study conducted by Mike Schultz, publisher of raintoday.com, a company that works with professionals to help them market their services, a key finding was the payoff received by authors who invested their own funds in the promotion of their books. In the study, 51% of the 200 authors who participated used their own money to back their book, the median investment being $4,500. The investments were typically used for hiring marketing or public relations firms, and the impact that these companies had on books' sales was significant.

The study found that authors who had outside help sold 10,000 copies of their first books and earned royalties of $55,000, compared to 4,500 copies sold and royalties of $25,000 for authors who depended entirely on the efforts of their publishers (excerpted, Publishers Weekly, April 24, 2006 by Jim Milliot).

Here are a few recommendations for reputable PR firms:

- authorbuzz.com: Offers authors a reasonable package deal for their services and has a proven track record.

- kruppkommunications.com: A dynamic New York public relations firm specializing in the creation of bulls-eye publicity for authors, celebrities, entertainers, CEOs, and corporations.

- cavehenricks.com/about.html: Owner Barbara Henricks' well-seasoned publishing public relations background has afforded her representation of such luminaries as Jack Welch, Maria Bartiromo, and Larry Bossidy. The firm is based in Austin, TX.

- goldbergmcduffe.com: Founded by Lynn Goldberg and based in New York City, has brought many authors to the bestseller list, including Jodi Picoult, John Bogle, Sandra Brown, and Maurice Sendak.

29 | Choosing the Right Publicist or PR Firm

When looking for a publicist or PR firm, start by asking your publisher for recommendations. Tell your editor what you're budgeting for publicity and they will be able to refer you to several publicists or PR firms that will suit your financial plan.

If you still can't find anyone who fits into your budget or meets your expectations, then contact writers' conferences, other writers, writers' associations, or do some Internet research. There is a slew of publicists out there who would be thrilled to work on your book; however, the "right" publicist is the only one you want.

In order to know what to expect from the publicist or PR firm you're hiring, have them submit a publicity plan for your book, along with a list of references. Their plan should include:

- Media outlets/contacts they intend to pitch to
- Length of time they will devote to publicizing your book
- Likely number of media hits they plan to achieve
- Press release (electronic and hard copy)
- Fee structure for their agreed involvement

If you are hiring a firm, inquire as to who specifically will be your contact and the person responsible for driving publicity on your behalf. It is important to build a good working relationship with your publicist—the more they understand about you and your book, the better they will be at pitching it and booking media.

Updates on the publicist's progress can come weekly, biweekly, or monthly, depending on the terms of your contract. He or she needs to submit an account of everyone contacted and the responses received (this includes media sources and dates); however, don't count on your publicist to reveal the names of their media contacts, as these are, in most cases, proprietary, and they will want to protect their relationships.

As always, the Internet is a great resource if you want to throw a wide net in your search for the appropriate publicist or firm to hire, but be sure to ask for references and proof of their claims to be able to garner publicity for your book.

30 | Who Will Handle Your Book's Publicity?

Whether you choose to employ your own publicist or to do the publicity work yourself, consider first if the publisher is providing publicity support for your book. Most titles will get a minimum of a press release and submission to local or national media. The amount of publicity attention that the publisher will give you is determined by the forecasted unit sales (copies) for your book. If your title is considered an "A-level" release, then you will most likely receive the maximum attention from your publisher's in-house publicity department. If your title falls in the mid-to-low range of releases, then you will most likely receive the minimum attention, in which case, you may benefit from hiring your own publicist.

Meet with and interview public relations firms and freelance publicists and consult with your publisher about your findings. Depending on the cost involved, it might be beneficial to hire a private publicist instead of a public relations firm, as you will receive individual attention and the cost will be significantly less overall. Again, be sure to conduct a thorough reference check before hiring anyone.

Many PR firms and individual publicists specialize in particular areas of the book genre market. It can be advantageous to hire someone who has an established reputation with the media regarding your title's genre, as he or she can more easily access the appropriate media contacts. For example, if you're a culinary author, then you shouldn't hire a publicist whose area of focus has been predominately in the business category.

The PR firm or publicist needs to be able to effectively lay out a publicity campaign for your book and provide examples of other successful book launches that they have worked on in the past. Accessing their past clients is a great way of authenticating their claims of success. They should be able to supply you with referrals.

Book publicity requires an entirely different skill set than other types of publicity. While publicists have similar attributes, it behooves you to engage a book publicist or PR firm. Think about it: Would you go to a general teacher to maximize your knowledge of mathematics, or would you seek out a mathematician? They both know how to teach math, but who is the expert? That's who you want to handle your book campaign—the book publicity expert. It's extremely important to hire the best that your budget permits.

31 | Hire Yourself as Publicist

Another approach is to do your own publicity. Tireless self-promotion can generate attention for your title and produce the desired outcome. It won't be free, but it will be less expensive than hiring someone to work for you. The biggest cost factor will be your time. Pool your resources and call in favors from friends, family members, and associates. If you have people to whom you can delegate tasks, you'll cover a lot more ground than you would on your own.

The first order of business is to create a knockout press release and kit. This should include the following information:

- Immediate release date: When the book will be available in your warehouse
- Contact information: Whom do you want the press to contact for interviews or more information? If you are the contact, list your contact options, including email and phone.
- Title, ISBN, retail price, publisher, date of publication (two to three weeks after warehouse receipt)
- Author bio
- Synopsis of the book
- Table of Contents
- Key items, highlighted: Does your book profess ten easy steps to...? Does the protagonist transform his or her life? How?
- Sample chapter
- Prior speaking schedule, if applicable, or potential speaking agenda. This reinforces your commitment to the sale of the book and will act as social proof for the public's demand of your message.
- A list of questions and answers that can provide more background information about you and your book.
- Sampling of any articles, essays, op-eds, or interviews (for current or previous books)

Most media outlets will accept an electronic press release (EPK) or hard copy press kit, but be sure to check before sending anything out. Also, sending a hard copy backup along with the book itself will attract attention and give you another reason to follow up.

You might want to consider hiring someone to write your press materials. As the author, remaining objective can be challenging. Most publicists would be happy to do this for a fee.

Once you've created your press materials, it's time to distribute them to the media. Start by contacting local media. This includes television stations, radio stations, newspapers, and magazines (look online for local listings). Once you've made contact and have been directed as to how to submit a press release or book an interview, you're on your way to building a grass-roots campaign.

32 | Timing of Publicity

When coming up with a publicity plan, begin by assessing who you're targeting. Are you going after print media, television (local, cable, or national), radio (local, public, sponsored, or national), or Internet outlets (blogs, sites, social media)? All of these media have precise timing protocols.

Print publications' time lines can be broken down as follows: Long-lead magazines work six-to-nine months out. If your book will be released in May and it's perfect for a Christmas or holiday-oriented publication, you should approach the magazine in March or April at the latest. Newspapers work on a shorter lead time due to the nature of the product. That said, allow at least a month or more for local papers and a few months for national papers.

For broadcast television, plan on pitching at least two-to-three months prior to your book's publication, depending on the show. Local or cable shows have a much shorter lead time than national shows and may offer to interview you with a month's notice. It's difficult to get national media attention, but if you don't ask, then you'll never know. Contact producers of shows that have a "fit" with your book's subject matter. Utilize the same methods of contact that you would for local media.

Radio stations can respond even faster than television stations. Plan to contact them, though, at least a month in advance.

While the Internet is instantaneous, the timing will depend on to whom you are pitching. Bloggers, websites, and social media outlets have their own specific criteria for interviews and mentions.

33 | Targeted Media List

Hiring someone who has an extensive targeted media list and who will also distribute your press release can prove to be very sensible, as it will maximize your publicity outreach and expedite the process.

If you would prefer to create and/or distribute your press release yourself, here are some resources to help you do that:

Creating a press release:

- press-release-writing.com/content-basics.htm: PRW has an excellent reputation and provides handy press release writing guidelines and samples.
- pr.com/rss-feeds: Many PR agencies are using RSS feeds.

Distributing a press release:

- us.cision.com
- mediacontactspro.com
- tvaproductions/com/mediaoutlets
- burrellesluce.com

Securing media attention can be achieved indirectly as well. There are numerous ways to generate publicity, including appearing at local bookstores, schools, libraries, hospitals, nursing homes, daycare centers, churches, or just about anywhere that you can create a "story" that ties into your book's topic. Be creative—think outside the pages and send an email "news alert" to the local press about your upcoming appearances (note: be sure to get permission from the hosting venue prior to contacting the press, as some may not allow media on the premises).

34 | Media Appearances Prior to Your Book's Release

Ideally, media bookings should take place at the time of your book's release. Timing is critical, which is why your publisher will advise you to delay media bookings until your book is close to release or has been recently distributed. If the media hits too early, that is, before the book hits the shelves, then the media may have little to no impact on the sale of your book. News tends to dwindle quickly as consumers move onto the next hot topic. If you have no choice but to accept a media appearance because it's the only interview the outlet can offer, the interviewer may allow you to mention that you have a new book. If this is the case, your publisher can supply the outlet with a digital image of your book's jacket to be included on the station's website or in your interview.

The right media can catapult your book to a bestseller list, resulting in increased sales, more book contracts, and more media attention. Therefore, don't waste the attention when your book isn't yet available for purchase. Because local press has a shorter lead time than national press, local media outlets may be more flexible in scheduling your interview or appearance closer to the publication date.

35 | Publication Window

"Pub date" refers to the date when your book is officially released and distributed and becomes available at book retailers and other outlets (this includes brick and mortar stores and online stores).

Media exposure and events are scheduled around your pub date; however, the publicist's planning and pitching has been going on for at least four months prior to this date. The publisher wants to ensure that the book will be available to customers when the media attention begins. If media attention happens prior to the book's availability, then there is a risk that that attention will not be effective in driving traffic to purchase your book. Depending on the location of the publisher's warehouse (the DC), it can take up to three weeks for a book to be fully disseminated from coast to coast.

The "pub window" usually extends three months out from the pub date and refers to the time during which the publisher puts its attention on garnering media attention, booking speaking appearances, and generally promoting your book; however, most media attention will likely take place during the first six-to-eight weeks following the book's release. Some books will receive media attention even up to a year or two after their releases due to promotion by someone of notoriety. For example, Echkart Tolle's book, *A New Earth*, was published in 2005 and selected by Oprah in 2008 for a webcast event with the author. As a result, the book became an overnight bestseller.

(As a side note about Oprah: Most authors want to be on her show and, unfortunately, very few ever get that privilege. If you're working with the publisher's in-house publicist or an outside PR firm, trust that they have the contacts for Oprah's producers and will submit your book to them, as long as it has a good chance of being selected. If they don't believe that your book has a chance, then trust their judgement— there is a lot at stake when publicists pitch to Oprah or any other big show. Publicists have relationships to protect and don't want to jeopardize their connections by pitching a book that they feel certain will be of no interest.)

The publisher typically will not continue to focus on titles much beyond the standard pub window because of all of the new releases (remember: over 275,000 books are released each year through traditional publishers) and because the press tends to only be interested in a title when it first hits the market.

36 | The Publicist Is No Longer With Your Publisher

Unfortunately, it sometimes happens that your pub-licist will leave your publishing house. As the author, there isn't really a whole lot you can do about this. The publisher is providing you a service, so trust their opinion that the replacement assigned to your book is competent and will do a great job of pitching your book to the press. If you are concerned, make that known to your editor to ensure that they are in the loop and will monitor the new publicist's efforts.

Set up an appointment with the new publicist to acquaint them with you and your book. You know your book better than anyone else, and the publicist has as much to gain by connecting with you as you do with them. The publicist's position is an integral part, if not the biggest part, of the book campaign. Make every effort to align yourself with him or her and offer your assistance. Make yourself available for interviews whenever possible, as this will further your chances for more of them.

Make sure to keep in mind that the publisher intends to do their best in representing your title, as it's in their best interest to do so. One of the hardest things for an author to do is to "let go" and trust that the publisher knows the marketplace and how to generate maximum media coverage while always maintaining a "watchful eye."

37 | Galleys, Bound Manuscripts, Blads, and Press Releases

The publicity department has access to an array of support materials for your book, including:

- Galleys: Uncorrected, soft cover, pre-publication proof editions of your book. These are used by the publicity, events, and sales departments to generate early interest in your book. The number of printed galley copies varies from 50 to 300 or more. Because they are costly to produce, galleys are typically only printed for big books when the publisher feels confident that they will secure media attention and increase the "buy" from a major bookstore chain.

- Bound manuscripts: Uncorrected proofs printed on 8.5x11 paper and bound with a clear plastic or paper title sheet. They cost less to produce than galleys and are generated upon request by publicity or sales in the event that galleys will not be created.

- Blads: Stands for book layout and design. They contain a brief, yet enticing overview of the book that's being published. They contain excerpts and may have a color front and back cover replicating the book's jacket. They will include the ISBN, publisher information, release date, and retail price (this same information is also included in galleys and bound manuscripts). Quantities produced depend on the overall publicity plan for the book, but can be as many as several hundred or more. Because of their small size, blads are a great sales support piece to be used as handouts at speaking engagements and quick references for media outlets.

- Press releases: Informational, persuasive selling tools for the publicist. They include the author's bio, past media appearances, speaking agenda, synopsis of the book, and publicist's contact information. Publishers create press releases for most of their publications.

38 | Op-Eds, Articles, and Essays

Op-eds, articles, and essays are considered means of publicity for your book. These methods are usually generated by the rights department within the publishing house and have the power to further a book's attention and sales. Ask your editor which department, rights or publicity, will be pursuing these media opportunities for your book.

An op-ed (short for "opposite the editorial page") is a newspaper article that is written by and expresses the opinion of an author who is usually not attached to the newspaper's editorial board. An article is a piece of nonfiction prose that works as an independent part of a publication. Authors may be invited to write an article for a magazine, newspaper, or website based on the topic of their book. Essays are typically short pieces of writing and are often written from an author's personal viewpoint.

Offering to contribute to a newspaper column or writing an essay, article, or op-ed will add to your credibility as perceived by your readers.

39 | Online Reviews

You may be familiar with book reviews published in newspapers or magazines, but have you ever considered pitching your book for reviews online? Start locally with any professional, membership-based, corporate, and alumni organization that you are associated with and send them a press release and copy of your book to see if they would be willing to mention it in their newsletter, journal, or magazine online. Perhaps they might mention your book on their website or feature it on their home page.

Remind your family members and friends to visit their favorite online book retailer and post positive reviews about your book. Online reviews don't have to be lengthy—a few sentences will do just fine. The more reviews you're able to gather, the more attention there will be for your book.

Pitch your book to specific online magazines and newspapers. Many hard copy publications publish online versions. The online editions may differ from their subscription or newsstand editions, offering added review coverage. As with any publication, online reviews are seen by other media outlets and will result in additional attention.

40 | The Power of Bloggers

Online media is on the rise and will continue to hold a viable and valuable share of the press coverage for your book. Bloggers (web loggers) are, in some ways, viewed as being as valuable as some key television, radio, or print journalists. Key bloggers who have followings on prominent websites or who have popular blog sites of their own (for example, The Huffington Post, Boing Boing, and Engadget) can move hundreds, if not thousands, of books by reviewing or mentioning them.

The following are sites that will help you find blogs that could be beneficial in your book campaign:

- technorati.com/pop/blogs: Technorati tracks the top one hundred blogs in the blogosphere.
- blogsearch.google.com: Google's blog-tracking service.

Blogs are arranged with the most recent posts appearing at the beginning. An active blog will be updated at least weekly and sometimes much more often. The number of comments and updates posted indicate whether or not a particular blog is being read and how popular it is. Typically, the more comments and updates, the more popular the blog.

How and where do you find bloggers? CyberJournalist (cyberjournalist.net) offers a comprehensive list of journalists' blogs. Approach lead bloggers through email about setting up an interview on their blog or posting a chapter, excerpt, or review. While contacting bloggers might seem simple, your request could be read as "spam." Be genuine in your approach and only reach out to relevant blogs.

Connecting with blogger communities (a form of social networking) is proving to be a very effective method of reaching the masses. Bloggers have the power to generate buzz about you and your book and should be considered a top priority when developing your promotional campaign.

41 | Electronic Press Materials

The media frequently request high-resolution author photos and images of book jackets. These can be posted on and downloaded from your publisher's website, which makes the process simple and quick for the press. Your publicist can also send electronic sample chapters, graphics, or author videos quickly and easily.

Publishers are making their catalogs available in digital format, which allows the press to obtain title and author information on a moment's notice. This also allows the media to respond quickly to titles of interest and to request review copies instantaneously.

Many publishers also have an online "press room" in which they feature press releases, author videos, author appearances, interviews, and upcoming author events.

42 | Publicity After the Pub Window

Your book has been in the marketplace for about three months and has had a good media run. You and your publicist have been successful in scheduling press bookings with national and local television and radio stations, magazines, and newspapers. By everyone's standards, you've had terrific publicity support. Congratulations! But what happens now?

As was mentioned previously, the media is most interested in books from the time they hit the bookstores to about six-to-eight weeks following release. Yes, there are exceptions, but your book may not have anything beyond the usual claims to fame than any other author's book. Your publisher has just informed you that they have exhausted all of their media contacts and feel that you've had a good campaign. The publicist will wrap up your publicity campaign and send you a "good-bye" letter listing the media events that took place and giving you guidance on what you can do on your own to continue the momentum. He or she will also ask your permission to pass on any queries from the media about your book directly to you or an outside publicist, should that be the case. Beyond the three-month pub window, the publicist will generally continue to send out review copy requests for up to six months after the pub date.

The publisher must move onto the next season's titles, so at this point, you and/or your outside publicist are on your own, so to speak. Unless there's a compelling reason, it is just not possible for the publisher's publicity department to "carry" an author for more than three months. A compelling reason might be that there has just been breaking news related to your topic and you are the perfect spokesperson for the subject. As long as the news remains "hot," the publicist may continue to pitch you; however, once that headline dissipates, so will his or her involvement in reaching out to the press on your behalf.

So, what can you and/or your outside publicist do to continue the press attention for your book? Follow up with local press outlets and offer to speak on a diverse number of topics that are related to your book. If your book is about motivation or management, there might be opportunities for you to offer your consulting services to your local cable station's staff, which could turn into additional coverage for your book.

Continue to schedule speaking engagements based on your book's topic. Many venues have their own press contacts and will notify the media about your appearance. Speaking will enable you to continue to push for your book's publicity and create additional sales.

When following up with local media, pitch yourself as a local expert on your topic or a related subject. You could just end up with your own newspaper column as a result of the great press coverage you received during your book's campaign. If you pay attention to current affairs, local community groups' and associations' happenings, and local politics, your book can be used to open media doors after the pub window. In other words, you might be viewed as a local celebrity because of your book and the press coverage it has already received. While the national media may be on to the next big book, you can capitalize on your book's momentum by reconnecting or establishing contacts with the local press.

Does your book have another angle or "spin" that wasn't pitched to the local or national media? For example, your book covers backyard bird-watching in the Northeast. Did your publicist offer to have the press visit your own backyard or a member of the press' backyard? Did you think to incorporate a book party in your backyard, supplying binoculars, a bird identification application for everyone's iPhone, and birdseed goodie bags? How about collaborating with the local garden or birdseed store to arrange a bird-watching expedition for the media only?

43 | Distinctive Ways to Approach Media

Being noticed by the press might be the biggest challenge you will face (other than having your book published in the first place). The media looks for "hooks" or "angles" that they can spin to make a good story even better.

The following are a few ideas to help you start brainstorming about the spin that you can put on your book to increase your chances of grabbing the media's attention:

- What would be considered unique about you and/or your book?
- How is your book's topic relevant to current events? If your book aligns with the national or worldwide news of the day or week, then you can position yourself as an expert (provided you have the credentials to back it up).

- Does the topic of your book align with any talk show hosts' interests? Oprah, Montel, and Ellen are shows that regularly feature authors. Monitor their topics, past and present. Consider whether or not your book's message ties into any subject that they're passionate about.

- Do you have other talents that could enhance the media's interest in your book? For example, some special needs authors have achieved notoriety because their unbelievable accomplishments in sports, inspiration, or the financial sector makes their "angle" unique. Also, consider your day job. Is your work related to your book's topic or something completely different? You can see how a school-teacher who has written a financial investment book might peak the media's interest.

- How can you package your book and bio in a way that makes an impression upon delivery to the press? (A word of caution here: While the media seeks out authors whose books are "new," they might not appreciate a quirky or weird approach. Be wise—ask trusted friends their thoughts about your ideas when it comes to how you make your package novel [no pun intended].)

You've probably noticed that at the heart of all of this advice is an emphasis on finding out what makes you notable among the hundreds of thousands of authors who are looking for media consideration. The media is very similar to publishers in that they are inundated with requests from a huge number of people, not just authors, who claim to have something newsworthy or publishable.

When publicists meet with the media, they literally have minutes to review an entire catalog of their publisher's titles per season. Sometimes, it can take something pretty dramatic to make you stand out. For example, if your book has a "smoking gun," that is, something not yet known about a popular public figure or incident, this could peak the press' curiosity enough to get you an interview.

Keep in mind that the media are competing to maintain and expand their following. The attractions that can influence viewers' (or readers' or listeners') emotions and persuade them to buy their publication or watch or listen to their program will ultimately win out over others because of their ability to gain advertising dollars. Media outlets are businesses like anything else—they require funding and loyal fan bases. Can your book boost a media outlet's audience?

44 | Your Own Radio Show

If you have what it takes to host your own radio show, there are many radio stations that are looking for programming. Can you develop a "radio voice" that will invite listeners to join you? If you don't have experience in speaking over the radio air waves, seek training.

The following are some resources to help you get your book's message out over the air:

- gumbopages.com/other-radio.html lists non-commerical radio stations, including Internet, Spanish-speaking, and international stations.

- Numerous college radio stations around the country have room in their broadcasting schedules. While students' music may tend to dominate their airwaves, most of these stations offer public affairs "talk" programs, and what better subject is there for such a program than an author's book topic?

- Contact public radio stations, which are funded by donations and often operated by volunteers. While these stations may have wait-lists for scheduling, a literary spot could be what they're looking for to satisfy a portion of their audience and to raise funding. Visit npr.org for a list of stations.

- You can also host your own radio show from home (keep in mind that this will require the purchase of some recording hardware and software). Your website will act as your sponsor and broadcast over the Internet or to subscribers through iTunes.

45 | Publisher's Sales and Marketing Support

Sales and marketing are essential to a successful book campaign and require collaboration between the publisher and author. Well-written text is the most important element of a book's success, but once the manuscript is complete, the author and publisher must focus on spreading the news about the book. This process is known as marketing, and everyone, including the author, must contribute to the book's promotion and sales. If you put as much effort into promoting your book as you did into writing it, then you'll be on your way to a winning campaign.

The publisher's marketing department will lead and implement the book's promotional plans as set forth by both them and the in-house sales support departments. They will oversee and allocate budget dollars as needed to further the sales of your book and are responsible for producing sales materials for the sales department, including sell-in tip sheets, kits, cover photos, catalogs, and sample book chapters. They also participate in trade shows and events related to the title's category and genre, arranging booth space where the publisher's related titles and printed materials are displayed. The marketing team conducts weekly sales meetings with the publicity team to check in on media bookings and also develop seasonal or title-specific promotions for the booksellers, increasing the sales force's chances of selling your book.

Your publisher may or may not have much room in the budget to support the sale of your book; it all depends on the projected sales volume for your title. As was mentioned earlier, big books get most of the attention, but it's all relative to the size of your publisher and the print run of your book.

46 | Publisher's Advertising Support

Depending on the print run of your book, the publisher may be able to provide a budget for advertising your book's release. One of the ways that a publisher can do this is through the bookstores. Most bookstores have a co-op account with their publisher, which represents a percentage of the bookstores' purchases that can be used to promote any of the publisher's titles; however, the publisher and the bookseller have to agree on how the money is spent and on which titles.

Advertising on local television and radio stations and in local publications may produce greater results than advertising in national outlets would. The cost of advertising regionally versus nationally is drastically different, and unless the publisher considers your book worthy (meaning it's a good investment of their dollars), chances are you'll be lucky to even get local ad support. Effective ads must run repeatedly and therefore require a hefty budget in order to produce good results. Publishers may select from a variety of methods to promote your book, including billboards, in-store signage, bus stop signage, or phone booth posters, just to name a few.

Radio ads are worthwhile for the right books (business books in particular work well on radio) and are geared toward the "drive-time" audience. Keep in mind, however, that radio advertising is similar to print advertising in that the ads need to be repetitive in order to have any impact that will translate into book sales.

Banner ads on related topics' websites are being utilized effectively and in some cases, depending on the book's audience, are the promotional method of choice. Just about any book can benefit from a banner ad, but some of the most popular ones are targeted toward women. Parenting tips, family budgeting, family vacations, and selecting a nanny are topics that usually fare well with banner ad support.

Online bookstores offer special placement (co-op dollars are used) on their website's homepage, topic/category pages, or as an "add-on" sale for customers purchasing another book that may be related (have a look at barnesandnoble.com or amazon.com to see examples of this).

Due to the progression of online promotion, print advertising is experiencing a steady decline. Online advertising is being booked at a rate of two-to-one against more traditional advertising methods, including magazines, newspapers, television, and radio. The cost of online promotion amounts to about a third of those more traditional methods and the coverage is targeted and expansive.

47 | Publisher's Collateral Marketing Materials

Sell-in kits, tip sheets, fliers, bookmarks, and brochures are just a sampling of the hard copy materials that the publisher's marketing department may produce to promote awareness of your book. These marketing materials are intended as promotional giveaways for bookstores and other retail outlets that carry books. They are also used by the publisher's sales force in their book buyer presentations as leave-behind items aimed at keeping particular titles in the buyer's line of vision. Authors can also use these sales support materials as handouts at speaking engagements, planting seeds in the minds of audience members to persuade them to buy the book.

The sell-in kit is an integral part of the marketer's sales support collateral materials. The kit consists of a two-pocket folder with the book's cover image on the front and the sell-in materials inside. Sell-in materials include the book's cover image, sample chapters, and publicity and marketing plans. The kit can also include a speaking agenda, news clippings, and an extended author bio.

A tip sheet is the sales force's quick, one-page summation that provides a rundown of pertinent selling points about a book and its author. It is designed for ease of use in book buyer presentations and includes the following information:

- Author's brief bio
- Sales handles: who will want to buy this book and why?
- Brief book topic description
- List of published titles competing with this topic and those titles' sales history
- Author's previous published books and sales history
- Date the book will be in the warehouse, date it will be released, and publication date
- ISBN (international standard book number, located on the book with the bar code)
- Retail price
- Bookstore category
- Marketing plans
- Publisher contact information (editor, marketer, publisher, product line)

Creating the cover image is a painstaking endeavor, involving design, layout, concept, and culminating in the all-inclusive packaging of the book. The marketer is part of the team, along with the designers, that creates and develops the look and feel of the book. Once the marketers have the book cover images, they are printed and/or made available electronically for use by the sales, publicity, and events departments. Imagine how much more effective a sales rep's, publicist's, or events coordinator's presentation could be with the book's cover image.

Your book's cover image will also appear in the publisher's seasonal catalog alongside all of the pertinent information for book buyers, including marketing and advertising support and scheduled media and event venues, that will assist them in determining whether or not your title interests them enough to purchase the book for their stores.

48 | Publisher's Online Marketing Support

Your publisher may be willing to help you build the foundation for your book's online marketing campaign by supporting some of the following online promotional opportunities, provided your title is a lead title. Lead titles have greater print runs than other books on the publisher's list (the print runs can be upwards of 15,000 copies).

If your book qualifies for the publisher's support, then they may agree to some of the following:

- Purchasing an email list related to your book's topic
- Helping you create a website
- Creating links to yours and/or the publishers' websites on related sites
- Advertising and promoting your book on related websites
- Funding and producing a video for placement on YouTube, Google Video, or Buzzbooster.com

Many publishers are also utilizing the services of Turn-Here (turnhere.com) to create two-minute video spots of their lead authors. These videos, while owned by the publisher, are available for other sites to link or use in any form, are fully accessible to retail outlets, and can be used by authors on their own websites.

The BookReporter.com (bookreporter.com) is a company that operates book publishing-related websites. While their services are not free, the company is worth looking into, as it reviews and promotes books through its newsletter (for which advertising is available for purchase). As an author, it's a good idea to register for this site and others in order to stay on top of how and what publishers are doing to promote their books. This is especially helpful if you're a one-man-band operation, as mirroring publishers' marketing efforts will assist you with your own.

Also, the marketer may assist you by providing jpegs, tif files, or other electronic files related to your book that you can use on your website, blog, Facebook page, and other online outlets.

The Internet continues to have a huge impact on our daily lives, and the promotional opportunities that it offers extend beyond our imaginations. Your book's online campaign will reap the many rewards of potentially hundreds of thousands of viewers and can produce mega book sales.

49 | Publisher's Sales Reps' Support

The publisher will present your book to the sales force at various times throughout the planning of the book's campaign and during the book's three-month pub window. The marketing, publicity, and sales teams meet weekly, biweekly, or monthly and also convene at seasonal sales conferences in which the marketers, editor, and publisher present the upcoming season's list of titles.

Internal updates via email or weekly "flash" reports boasting publicity hits and events bookings are distributed to the sales reps so that they can use the up-to-the-minute campaign news to enhance their sales of a particular title. When a rep has trouble convincing a buyer to purchase a title (or to purchase a significant quantity of a title), publicity and events bookings can sometimes sway that buyer to reconsider his or her position.

Sales reps are asked to provide feedback from their buyers to the marketing team in order to create and deliver the best possible book package. Buyers' input is priceless and has the power to change a book's cover, title, price, and delivery date. The sales team takes a proactive approach to selling a book, scheduling regular meetings with their customers in order to gain that feedback.

It might be beneficial to ask if your publisher's sales department is in-house or outsourced, as this can determine how aggressive and effective their efforts are in relation to the volume of book sales that they generate. Because in-house sales teams are governed by their publishers and, for that reason, have their jobs at stake, in-house teams tend to be more beneficial to the author. Freelance sales firms, on the other hand, have more than one client, and therefore, more than one source of income, which can leave room for slacking off.

Being published by a traditional publisher carries a huge advantage when it comes to selling your book to all of the bookselling retailers. There is absolutely no way for an individual author to contact the thousands upon thousands of possible retail establishments, nor would the majority of these bookstore buyers meet with an author. The traditional book publisher is responsible for planting your book in the retail outlets.

Self-published authors must rely on their books being selected from a catalog or on presentations by the self-publisher's sales reps to wholesale distributors. The wholesalers are then responsible for selling these titles to bookstores. Traditional bookstores will purchase self-published books from wholesalers, but usually only upon request. Also, they do not have face-to-face meetings with self-publishers' sales reps.

50 | Location of Your Book on the Bookstore's Shelves

The location of your book within the bookstore is determined by its categorization. Your book's genre and category will be determined by your publisher; however, if your book falls under more than one category, the bookstore buyer might request that the publisher classify it differently than originally planned. For example, a parenting book that deals with running a home business and being a successful parent simultaneously might qualify to be shelved on both the business shelf and the parenting shelf. In such an event, the publisher and the buyer will determine what they think will be the most saleable location and then code the title accordingly.

Imagine that one or two copies of your book are on the shelf, but you'd like it to be displayed in greater quantity on an end cap shelf (these are the shelves that run perpendicularly to the long-running bookstore shelves), at the front of the store, in the store's window, on the "New Release" shelf, or at the cash wrap. Each of these locations is considered "special" and requires that the publisher pay for the privilege of housing your title there.

The bookstore's purchases accumulate a percentage of sales dollars that is held in an account called a "co-op." This gives the bookstore a bank account to use for the promotion of your book and others released by a given publisher. It's up to the buyer and the publisher's representative to determine the optimum use of these co-op dollars. If they agree that one of these special placements will boost the sale of your book, then they will establish a time frame during which your book will be housed in two locations (both its category space and its special location). This decision is partly based on the most effective use of the store's real estate. If your book turns quickly, then it's likely that the publisher and the bookstore will agree to extend this time frame. The publisher might also offer a promotional discount for your book, which would encourage the bookseller to place it outside of its normal location. On the other hand, if the special location doesn't further the sale of your book as predicted, then it will probably be moved back to its categorical shelf. Your publisher and the bookseller will consider the following factors when determining whether or not your book qualifies for special placement:

- Does it tie in with current affairs?
- Is it receiving a lot of publicity?
- Is it on special promotion?
- Is it a bestseller?
- Do you have an upcoming appearance?

The location of your book on a store's shelves will be determined based on that store's schematic, which is a very detailed plan that takes into account every inch of the store. In the schematic, individual categories are broken down into sections and sub-sections. For example, the nonfiction area will contain numerous categories, including business, self-help, religion, cooking, travel, and more. The sub-sections of these might include, respectively, finance, motivation, Catholicism, vegetarian cooking, and Europe.

51 | Promotional Expenses Covered by the Publisher

The days of publishers sending authors on twenty-city book tours are pretty much long gone (with the exception of celebrity authors); however, there are still ways in which the publisher might consider offering financial support to your title. Here are just a few promotional expenses that your publisher may deem worthwhile:

- Most publishers will at least provide the author with fliers, bookmarks, chachkas, or other printed support materials for the release of the book.
- If the book is considered top-tier, then the publisher might provide advertising dollars to promote the title's release, through web and print ads, the purchase of email blast lists targeting niche audiences, billboards, and more.
- Some publishers will send authors on a limited tour of cities, covering transportation, food, and lodging.
- Some publishers will pay for a book launch reception.
- The publisher's publicity department will usually send out review copies or a press release.
- Some publishers will cover the costs of speaking engagements at bookstores or other small venues.

Publishers' budgets for book promotion can range anywhere from a few hundred dollars to thousands of dollars; how much your book will receive depends on both the size of the publisher and the salability of your book as determined by your publisher. Keep in mind that, as with other promotion and publicity-related efforts, the marketing of your book will rely on your own manpower, too. This means that, as you have become accustomed to wearing a variety of hats with the publishing of your book, this particular hat needs to remain a permanent fixture on your head. A smart author is always ready and eager to sell his or her book. Have a copy of your book with you at all times—you never know whom you're going to meet.

52 | "Live" Author Appearances

There are numerous live event outlets to be considered when coming up with a promotion plan for your book. As the name would suggest, live events involve presenting or speaking about your book in front of an in-person audience. A live event can also entail presenting a lecture or talk via the web through a webinar, teleseminar, or podcast. Referring to a live audience helps to distinguish your promotional events, which may consist of media appearances in which your audience is remote and not in "real time."

Selecting the right event forum and venue for your book is fundamental to its success in terms of sales, promotion, and publicity. Boosting these three factors is the main goal of any promotional event, and while all three of them might not be the main focus of an event, they all must be brought into the equation when choosing and scheduling your book-related engagements. Ultimately, it's all about maximizing your time in order to produce the optimum results in book sales.

A question to ask yourself before you jump into arranging speaking appearances is whether or not public speaking is something you enjoy doing. Many authors write well, but when it comes to getting up in front of a live audience, they are either completely uncomfortable or don't know what to say. This will result in a poorly-delivered book talk and decrease book sales opportunities.

If you just lack the experience but are comfortable speaking, then it may be beneficial to join a Toastmasters group, hire a private speaking coach, practice your delivery in front of a mirror, or video tape your talk. Any of these means of perfecting your book talk will be beneficial, and preparation will make the experience more enjoyable for you.

If after evaluating your comfort level and your desire to speak publicly, you determine that this medium of spreading the word about your book isn't for you, then you might want to look into some of the social media venues, which are gaining in popularity and are accessible internationally to anyone with a computer, cell phone, or MP3 player.

53 | Bookstores

Bookstores are often referred to in the publishing industry as "brick and mortar." These days, bookstores range in size anywhere from a few hundred square feet to thousands of square feet.

There are independent bookstores and national bookstores. Independent bookstores are stores owned and operated by individuals in a particular local region. They can be concentrated in a community or city or they may have a chain of stores in several states. These stores are often proprietary and family-owned and operated. Several top-tier independent bookstores include Book Revue, Joseph Beth Booksellers, Tattered Cover , Book Passage, Changing Hands, and Politics and Prose. For a complete list of independent booksellers in the United States, check out newpages.com/bookstores/default.htm.

National bookstores include Barnes & Noble and Borders. These stores have bookstores throughout the United States and abroad and operate as corporations. There are also regional bookstore chains, including Books-A-Million and Hastings, that are located in specific areas of the U.S.

Many independent bookstores belong to the professional organization known as The American Booksellers Association (ambook.org/index.html). The ABA has established its own bestseller list and receives submissions from its members. It also offers its members promotional, educational, and technological support. The ABA has resources for its members that the independent bookseller wouldn't otherwise, in some cases, be able to access or afford. The ABA is highly regarded in the publishing industry and is very influential among publishers and booksellers.

54 | Meeting Your Local Booksellers

If you have a local independent or national bookstore in your community, introducing yourself and making yourself known may help to drive book sales. Most neighborhood bookstores are happy to support local authors. Ask if they would be willing to host an appearance and/or a launch party for you for your book. Provided the store is capable, well-staffed, and has the physical space, they typically will be more than agreeable. After all, they want customers in their store, and having an author speak will generally bring them in.

Please understand that the bookstore knows their clientele better than you do and will be able to advise you as to whether or not your subject matter will attract a sizable audience (twenty-five or more attendees). This is part of the bookstore's criteria for agreeing to schedule an author appearance. Generally, bookstores' most popular event book topics are in the fiction category and include the genres of romance, comedy, drama, mystery, sci-fi, adventure, and children's. The nonfiction categories of memoir, motivation, inspiration, cooking, or instruction (crafts, decorating, or gardening) can also produce a favorable turnout, provided the author has a following (fan base). Of course, there are always exceptions. If you happen to possess "expert" status on a particular subject, or if your book's topic ties into current affairs, or if you are a well-known local author, then it's likely that your appearance will generate a sizable audience.

When contacting a bookstore for an appearance, always remember to be respectful and friendly. An over-zealous approach will most likely result in a lack of attention for you, your book, and a subsequent loss of sales. If you ask a bookstore to host an event and they decline, it's best to thank them for their consideration and move on. Pressuring the bookstore staff to host an appearance will only alienate you in the future when you may have a book that will be appealing to their customers.

55 | The Successful Bookstore Event

The success of a bookstore event is determined by the number of attendees, books sold, promotional opportunities, and amount of publicity generated by both you and the bookstore. Here are some helpful questions to ask and things to consider as you prepare for your bookstore event:

- Ask the bookstore what they consider a "successful" author appearance to be. Ordinarily, a bookstore will be pleased if they have twenty-five to forty or more attendees and sell the book to half of them. As you can imagine, they are aiming for the greatest number of attendees, since having more people present can automatically increase book sales.

- What will the bookstore do to support your appearance? As a rule, a successful event will require more than just a listing of your upcoming event in their newsletter. It will require in-store promotion, window signage, an email blast, a newsletter announcement, advertising, the author's own invitation to those on his/her guest list, and fliers being made available to local merchants, libraries, and schools. Many bookstores will do all of this and more. Because reaching out to the local media can help bookstores broaden their audience and pull in attendees from beyond the local community, some may contact television and radio stations or the newspaper to set up author interviews.

- Contact the bookstore at least two-to-three months in advance of your desired event date. This will allow enough time for the bookstore to promote your engagement.

- Be prepared to provide the bookstore with a guest list. Today, most bookstores will prefer an email list. If you don't have an email list compiled, create one. Emailing is the most expeditious mode of inviting people to attend your event. If you want to send a hard copy announcement as well, ask the bookstore for some of their printed newsletters and send those to your guests (most stores publish a store newsletter via an email blast or print).

- Ask if your local bookseller reports book sales to a bestseller list and which ones they contribute their sales information to. Bookstores are part of a grassroots book campaign and can drive enough sales to get your title on bestseller lists. Getting on a "list" attracts additional media and helps drive future sales.

56 | Supporting Your Bookstore Appearance

Leaving nothing to chance for your upcoming bookstore appearance will serve you, the bookstore, and your audience well. The following checklist will help to remind you of the importance of every detail in order to guarantee the event's success:

- Review your speaking schedule two weeks ahead of time with your in-house publishing contact (events coordinator or publicist).

- If you're booking events on your own, contact the bookstore two weeks prior to make sure that they have received your book and are promoting your appearance (for example, do they have a poster in the window announcing your upcoming appearance?).

- Send out an email blast two weeks before, one week before, and the day before your appearance to your potential guests stating the date, time, and place. Be sure to include the title of your book, your bio, book synopsis, and why anyone would want to meet you and hear you speak.

- Blog about your upcoming appearance on related websites, starting a month prior to the event and extending up to days before it.

- Circulate fliers in local shops, libraries, churches, hospitals, and wherever your book may be of interest.

Attire and etiquette:

- Dress in a casual, but business-like manner. Be well-groomed.

- Men should be clean-shaven and have clean, combed hair.

- Ladies, if you've been thinking about a manicure, now is the time to have one. Fans will be in close proximity when you are autographing your book. Your hair should also be neat and clean.

- Arrive fifteen minutes prior to your scheduled event appearance.

- Greet the bookstore staff in a gracious manner; this will serve you long after the event.

- Many independent bookstores still hand-sell books. They will likely remember you in a favorable manner and recommend your book if you are a likable guest in their store.

The event itself:

- Observe where your book is located and the quantity they have on display. Remember that your book would not be massed out in quantity or have a prominent location in the store without your appearance.

- Ask the bookstore if they have someone who can take a few pictures while you're speaking and signing your book (don't depend on the store to have a camera available; instead, bring your own).

- Ask if the bookstore will record your appearance and upload it to their website. If so, they will need your approval and, of course, say yes!

- The bookstore will have a designated area where they host their authors. They will have a podium or table, a microphone, if necessary (large room, high ceilings, large audience), water, and a copy of your book on hand.

- The manager or events associate will introduce you. If you want to approve what will be said about you beforehand, provide the event organizer with a written introduction and/or bio ahead of time.

57 | Bookstore Presentation Tips

Most bookstore author appearance programs consist of twenty minutes of speaking by the author, twenty minutes of interactive question-and-answer, and twenty minutes of autographing. Of course, these times are approximate and vary according to the attendance. The following tips will help guide you through your appearance:

- After the introduction, thank the store for hosting you and thank the attendees for coming, then launch into why you wrote the book and any other information about your process.

- Give the audience a synopsis of the book, but leave out enough detail that they will feel compelled to buy it. You may also choose to read a selection from your book (this is customary for fiction authors).

- Keep an eye on the audience's reaction to what you're sharing, as this can indicate what peaks their interest. As a speaker, you have the capacity to lead, engage, and entertain your audience. An ability to read the audience's reaction will guide your presentation's focus.

- Hold your book up periodically and refer to content or information that you're not sharing in-depth with them today, but that can be found in your book. Don't overdo it, though—you don't want to turn anyone off with a sales pitch.

- After you've conveyed what you wish to the bookstore guests, open the floor for questions. The bookstore staff will facilitate the question-and-answer period, which usually lasts for about ten to twenty minutes.

58 | The Book Signing

Your book signing will immediately follow your talk, either in the space in which you spoke or in an adjacent area of the store. The bookstore staff will assist you in this process by organizing a controlled line, admitting one person at a time to approach you with their books to be autographed.

When all of the attendees have received their signed copies, offer to sign store stock. Any book signed by the author is considered "sold" and is typically non-returnable to the publisher (publishers allow the return of unsigned books, unlike most other retailers. This policy, however, is being reviewed and will likely change in the future). Persuade the bookstore to allow you to sign as many copies of your book as possible. Bookstores know the value of autographed copies and that they usually outsell unsigned copies.

After your event, send a hand-written thank you note to the bookstore's staff. These days, personalized notes show that you took a moment to recognize their efforts. If it's not possible to send a hand-written note, send an email immediately. Post a blog comment on the bookstore's website about your experience or comment on Facebook or Twitter. Any public mentions of gratitude and praise will put you in good stead for the future and encourage book sales by the bookstore's staff.

59 | Drive-By Book Signings

Discuss with your publisher organizing a series of drive-by bookstore signings. At a drive-by signing, you literally drive to and stop into the bookstore to sign its stock of your book. Keep in mind that many stores might not have enough copies of your book to make it worth your while. Some publishers will take the lead and arrange drive-by signings for you, while others may give you the approval to handle interactions with bookstores on your own. If that's the case and you're managing the signings, then start calling the bookstores within a thirty-to-fifty-mile radius of your home (or stores in locations to which you'll be traveling during the three-month publication window). In order to create a targeted list of potential stores, take a look at the following websites: newpages.com/bookstores/default.htm#index, storelocator.barnesandnoble.com, and borders.com/online/store/LocatorView.

When you contact a store, ask to speak with their events organizer, manager, or manager on duty. Tell them in ten seconds or less who you are and why you're calling. Let them know that you're going to be in the area and ask if you can stop by to sign their stock of your book. If they say yes, then arrange a time and contact person. Be gracious and commit to the appointment. Sign whatever book stock they offer (usually between three and ten copies). The store will place "autographed" stickers on the jacket of your book, which will draw attention and add value to them.

If the bookstore says no, then respect their decision and move on. The worst thing you can do is be pushy or argumentative. If you persist, they might contact your publisher, and this type of behavior could adversely affect the sale and placement of your book in their store.

Pass along the list of bookstores for which you'll be signing books to your publisher so that they can make sure that the bookstores will have your book on hand when you arrive. As with all of your appearances, live or virtual, timing is essential. Signed copies will sell best early on in your book's release (within the first six-to-eight weeks).

60 | Events with Local Organizations

Author presentations can be beneficial to all kinds of organizations. An author appearance can serve as a means of spreading awareness of an organization, thereby increasing its membership or earning it media attention. Good groups to look for have strong community ties, access to the local press, and the resources to endorse an author and his or her book.

If you're not already a member of the Chamber of Commerce or other local community interest groups, joining at least one is a good idea, as these organizations can provide networking and promotional opportunities, which could ultimately mean extra sales for you. Some examples of successful organizational events include:

- Chamber breakfasts, luncheons, or receptions in which your book is included in the ticket price. These will help you to establish yourself in the business community.
- PTA meetings. Speaking and selling your book at monthly PTA meetings shows that you're concerned about the youth of the neighborhood.
- Urban Leagues or churches. Conducting a workshop or seminar for these organizations and having your book available for purchase by attendees will further your societal relationships.

All of these organizations will have similar methods of promoting your appearance and contacting the local media. Their promotional means may be limited due to a lack of funds, but they should all have a list of members whom they can contact via email, mail, or phone on your behalf.

Always remember to conduct yourself in a professional manner and offer your assistance in marketing your upcoming appearance. Also, allow at least three-to-six months' lead time in booking an event, as these outlets will need adequate time to make the announcement in their newsletters and meetings and to reserve a space to set up your event.

61 | Conferences or Conventions

An important thing to consider when booking yourself for an appearance at a conference or convention is lead time (or, the length of time preceding the event's opening date). Unlike bookstores and local organizations, conferences tend to cast much wider nets in order to reach the masses that might find their subject matter appealing. These conferences and conventions usually take place in hotels or convention centers, which requires that the organizations hosting them reserve the physical space far in advance. The amount of lead time can range from four to eighteen months (or sometimes, even longer).

Internet research on your book's topic should give you a good indication of which conferences or conventions are well-suited to your book. The exposure for you and your book can be amazing, as these conferences and conventions tend to have a very deep concentration of people interested in specific subject matter. Their promotion and publicity outreach is usually very thorough and they tend to utilize every imaginable means of getting the word out; however, the fact that they're called "conferences" and "conventions" doesn't certify that they will be professionally run and able to portray you in the best light. There is no substitute for researching, asking for references, and asking questions to ensure that a specific conference or convention is the correct place for you to speak about your book.

Often times, you can negotiate for your book to be included in the ticket price as an "added value" for the attendees. This also will allow the conference or convention to earn a few dollars since they will purchase your book at a wholesale price and advertise the retail value of your book within their promotions. The best thing about including your book in the ticket price is that the sale of your book is guaranteed. You may negotiate trading your speaker's fee for a definite number of books (one hundred or more, usually) purchased in this way, which ensures that, no matter how many people show up, you will sell a predetermined number of books.

62 | University Author Events

The speaking forums at universities include assemblies, alumni gatherings, homecomings, graduations, freshman orientations, fund-raisers, and more. Most publishers have well-developed relationships with universities and may be able to assist you in seeking an appearance that will be fruitful.

The advantage of speaking at a university about your book is that, if you are able to speak in front of the right faculty, you may be able to convince them to adopt your book as part of the curriculum. Of course, that means that you have researched the university's departments well enough to know that your book has enough of an educational angle and interest to be considered.

Keep in mind, though, that while you have opportunities within the university to promote your book and possibly have it adopted, its outreach is heavily concentrated within its confines. This doesn't necessarily mean that your appearance won't be promoted to the general public, but you should be aware of who the university will target in the marketing of your event. By doing this, yours and the university's expectations will be in alignment.

Lead time for booking an appearance may be tedious, as universities tend to have a committee process, which adds to the length of time to confirm an event. These committees usually meet on a specific day of the month, and while committee members see and talk to each other in between meetings, they have to maintain their committee approval process. Allow yourself at least three-to-six months' lead time.

Once you reach an agreement with the Student Affairs Administration or the Office of Development at the university, chances are you can pursue appearances at other campuses. As with other businesses, universities communicate with each other, which makes a recommendation from one university worth its weight in gold.

63 | Book Clubs

According to Ann Kent, founder of Book Group Expo, an annual gathering of readers and authors, there are around four-to-five million book clubs in the United States alone, and that number continues to increase (*The New York Times*, December 7, 2008).

How are books selected for book clubs? Bookstores, libraries, and individuals arrange book club meetings, and the books are chosen by the potential readers and the book club leader. Publishers also make recommendations to bookstores and libraries, but the final decision is made by the members of the book club.

Some authors appear either in-person or via telephone at book club meetings to chat about their book. An author's live voice can add to a dynamic discussion, keep the readers interested, and possibly cause them to consider reading other of that author's books. As an author trying to have your book selected for a book club, visit your local bookstores and libraries and offer to enhance their book club's meetings by appearing or calling in.

All book club members buy, borrow, or check out the books that they read, so being a book club pick translates to an almost guaranteed sale. The size of the clubs can range anywhere from a handful to twenty-to-thirty people. At the very least, book clubs serve as additional promotion for your book.

64 | Book Festivals and Fairs

Book festivals occur year-round all over the United States and are wonderful family outings. They generally attract from 2,000 to upwards of 35,000 people over a one or two-day period. Book festivals are promoted city and sometimes statewide. (More than likely, you or your publisher would never spend this kind of money promoting your book. We're talking thousands of dollars.) The festival organizers will have either a national bookseller such as Barnes & Noble or a local, independent bookseller on-site; however, book sales tend to be on the soft side unless your book is family-oriented. Nonetheless, books are sold and there is an autographing area for the authors to meet their fans.

Besides the tremendous opportunities for publicity and promotion inherent in book festivals, they allow you, the author, to be seen with your peers, contributing to a charitable family gathering. Festivals also present all kinds of opportunities for interviews by local television stations, newspapers, magazines, and radio stations.

Audience demographics at book festivals run the gamut, from local firefighters to CEOs to children. Some authors have been approached by company representatives to speak at a number of different venues, including company sales meetings, corporate commemorative celebrations, managers' motivational workshops, and more. Also, librarians organizing "meet the author" nights at their libraries attend book festivals to find their next authors to host. Book fairs and festivals can also serve as places to be "discovered," as publishers and agents scout them in search of up-and-coming authors to contract their stories.

Some well-known book festivals in the U.S. include The Miami Book Festival, The Baltimore Book Festival, The National Book Festival (former First Lady Laura Bush started this when George W. Bush took office), The Texas Book Festival, The Los Angeles Times Book Festival, The Big Read in St. Louis, and Black Books Galore Book Festival in NY, DC, and LA. Visit publishersweekly.com/article/CA6581379.html for a look at previous years' list of book festivals.

If you're up for some fun in the sun, meeting new authors, talking about your book, or a chance to see your name in the news, then look into book festivals that are happening in your area or places you may travel to in the future. Contact the fair's City Office of Promotion and The Arts or visit its website for scheduling details. Think ahead, as the lead time can be from four-to-six months prior to opening day.

65 | Book Expo of America

The publishing industry is host to numerous annual book expositions throughout the United States and abroad.

Book Expo of America (BEA) is the largest and only national publishing industry book expo in America. Many of the large and small independent publishers have booths that sponsor a number of author appearances, highlighting upcoming fall titles or newly-released titles. As in other retail markets, book sales are at their highest in the fall, so publishers utilize book expos to promote the newest and biggest titles.

Galleys, books, blads, bookmarks, posters, chachkas, and many other giveaway items are picked up by booksellers and librarians to either put in their stores or keep for themselves. It's not out of the ordinary to see a bookseller or librarian walking the showroom floor, followed by a pull-cart stuffed full of all the free stuff they landed.

There are also educational forums for booksellers, publishers, and authors, as well as special events, including author breakfasts, lunches, teas, receptions, and more. In order for an author to appear, he or she needs to be submitted by his or her publisher. If your publisher is not attending, it's unlikely that you will be able to participate in the scheduled programs; however, some authors have managed to book appearances on panels for educational programming and/or in the special author autographing area because of their celebrity status or personal relationships with organizers.

Booksellers from the United States and around the globe attend BEA expecting to see noteworthy authors, find out about books that have yet to be released, and to network with publishers. The BEA is attended by publishers from around the world, making it a great place to gain exposure for foreign sales and rights.

66 | Regional Book Expos

The size of publishers' booths at book expos is proportional to the size of the expos themselves. Because regional expos target smaller demographics and therefore take place in smaller spaces, publishers tend to have only a fraction of the space that's allotted to them at BEA. Despite their smaller size, however, regional expos offer programs for authors and publishers that are similar to those offered by BEA. Visit the website for your locale to learn how you can participate.

- New England Booksellers Association/NEBA: new-englandbooks.org

- The New Atlantic Independent Booksellers Association/NAIBA: naiba.com

- Mountains and Plains Independent Booksellers Association/MNBA: mountainsplains.com

- Great Lakes Booksellers Association/GLBA: books-glba.org

- Midwest Booksellers Association/UMBA: midwest-booksellers.org

- Southern Independent Booksellers Alliance/SIBA: sibaweb.com

- Northern California Independent Booksellers Association/NCIBA: nciba.com

- Southern California Independent Booksellers Association/SCIBA: scbabooks.org

- Pacific Northwest Booksellers Association/PNBA: pnba.org

Keeping your manners in check, present a press kit about yourself and your book to the show's organizers. Often, these shows are looking for authors to appear in an educational forum, whether it's a panel discussion, an interview by local media, or a keynote address. Your publisher may be willing to provide complimentary galleys or printed books for any of these forums. Be sure to notify your editor if you are speaking at a publishing industry trade show or program.

Like BEA, regional shows provide an opportunity for local bookstores and libraries to discover publishers' new title releases for upcoming seasons.

67 | Book Launch Parties

A book launch party is a celebration of your book's release that provides an occasion to share this momentous event with family, friends, and colleagues; however, its primary function is to draw out reporters. Your book's genre, venue, and budget will determine the type of reception, but the common element in most is that they're congratulatory gatherings. Many journalists look for just this sort of thing to report on for the local community and may be inclined to interview you and your guests about your book during the party.

The lead time for invitations to be sent, either in hard copy or via email, is a minimum of six weeks. Sending a save-the-date reminder eight weeks in advance is also helpful, as giving your invitees more notice will most likely increase turnout. Request the R.S.V.P. one week prior to the launch party's date. If your acceptance responses are not up to your expectations, sending a reminder notice two days prior to the event may produce additional guests.

Common locations for launch parties include the author's home, a friend of the author's home, a restaurant, bookstore, or church. Hosting your party at a well-known, exclusive restaurant or private club will improve your chances of attracting the press. Consult the calendar of local and national holidays in order to avoid conflicts in which the media would have to choose between your party and another affair.

If you're hosting your own launch party, ask your local bookstore to sell your book at the party. Allow the bookstore to bring their newsletter or other promotional materials to hand out with the sale of your book. This way, it becomes advantageous for the bookseller not only because they're selling the book, but also because the event becomes a promotional opportunity for the store itself.

At times, a publisher may support a launch party for its lead authors with the sole intent of attracting media. The publisher will often provide complementary copies of your book for guests and may also provide printed invitations and cover the costs of the rental space, food, and drinks. Still, there's no promise that the media will turn out—it's really a hit-or-miss proposition when counting on the press to show up.

No matter the venue, guest list, or number of books sold, the major reason to have a launch party is to obtain the media's interest. For that reason, be wise in choosing where and when to host the launch party. In addition, if you have any attending celebrity guests (local or national) behind your book, this may encourage the media's attentiveness.

An invitation includes:

- The name of the publisher or host
- The title of the book
- The date, time, and location of the reception
- RSVP date
- RSVP contact info, phone, and email address

One side of the invitation should contain the text and the other side should display a picture of your book jacket. This layout and design will enable you to create a postcard invitation, which can also serve as a flier for local shops.

68 | Speakers Bureaus

A speakers bureau is an agency that is in the business of providing professionals, experts, and/or celebrities who lecture on a given viewpoint. There are a number of speakers bureaus that select authors to present lectures on their books' content for live presentations.

If your book's idea is of importance to corporations, organizations, clubs, charities, special interest groups, and conferences, then contact a matching speakers bureau. Because there is a large number of bureaus to choose from, research the Internet for a bureau that fits your topic.

A few business-oriented bureaus include:

- Washington Speakers Bureau: washingtonspeakers. com
- National Speakers Bureau: nationalspeakers.com
- The Leigh Bureau: leighbureau.com

- Authors Unlimited: authorsunlimited.com

After you've established the right speakers bureau for you, send them an introductory letter or query, press kit, EPK (electronic press kit), and a link to your website. When you arrive at an agreement with a particular speakers bureau, before signing the contract, stipulate that your book must be present at or included in all of your speaking engagements. Most bureaus will not pay attention to this detail, as they make their commission on your speaking fee and not the book. It will be up to you to guarantee that your book is available for all of your engagements.

69 | The Benefits of Joining a Speakers Bureau

The overarching advantage to joining a speakers bureau is that they act on your behalf, generating income opportunities and additional book sales. Speaking adds to your platform as an author in the marketing and sales' support for your book and is highly regarded by your publisher. Speakers bureaus also take care of some administrative details, for example, negotiating your fees and travel expense coverage with the hosting venues.

Many authors are signed (or contracted) with a number of diverse speakers bureaus and make a nice living by doing so. Belonging to a speakers bureau can be a solid negotiating point with potential publishers, as it represents an additional avenue for the promotion of your book.

Speakers bureaus produce catalogs boasting the talents of their stable of speakers, have extensive websites that receive thousands of hits, and constantly advocate their speakers to every possible speaking outlet that pertains to their members' expertise. As an author, being among some of your peers at a speakers bureau will convey volumes about who you are and solidify your credentials.

Some publishers have started their own speakers bureaus or have partnered with existing ones, including:

- Penguin Speakers Bureau: penguinspeakersbureau. com
- Harper Collins Speakers Bureau: harpercollins-speakersbureau.com
- Random House partnered with American Program Bureau: randomhouse.com/knopf/ksb/speaker. php?sid=56

Keep in mind that, in order to be represented as a speaker with any publishing house, you must be one of their authors.

70 | "Live" Appearance Venue Attributes

Consider the topic of your book and then pitch it to appropriate venues that are known for hosting speakers. The best venues, on the whole, will offer to make your book available to the attendees. They may choose to buy your book and include it in the ticket price, thereby guaranteeing that a certain number of books are sold, or they might instead arrange to have a bookseller on-site or sell it themselves. At the very least, the venue will allow the author to sell his or her book at the back of the room.

Depending on the venue, your appearance will be publicized in a number of different ways, including on-premise signage, bulletin board notification, displays in common or reception areas, advertisements, email blasts, website announcements and blog posts, newsletter listings, and outreach to organizations, associations, clubs, and groups. Many will allow the media to attend free of charge, and some might have an in-house publicist who will pitch the possibility of interviews to the local media. Some may also offer complimentary tickets for your guests or preferred seating for members of the media.

71 | Online Events

The webinar has recently been and continues to be a prominent medium for author presentations. If you have yet to experience a webinar, research the Internet and you'll find an abundance of them, just begging for your participation.

The Internet-based webinar allows the speaker and participant to interact via the phone, email, or texting. This medium allows the author to act as if he or she is in front of an audience with the same (if one step removed) intimacy of being live.

In terms of sales, the admission ticket for a webinar is often a copy of the book, or the book is sometimes sold separately through the hosting venue. Hosting your own webinar can be done easily through a number of online chat providers, including, Skype (skype. com/welcomeback), Google, Yahoo!, and MSN. All you need is a webcam on your computer or a stand-alone webcam such as those offered by Logitech.

Teleseminar is an audio-only medium that requires participants to call in to a designated phone number and log on with an access code. This forum represents additional speaking opportunities for authors who are traveling and unable to access a computer. As was mentioned before, some authors contact book clubs via telephone while they're on the road, traveling between live appearances. Books can be purchased through the author's website, from online booksellers, or through the publisher directly.

A podcast is another medium through which to discuss your book's content; however, the content of the discussion will be static, since podcasts must be uploaded to a computer, iPod, or other compatible electronic device. Because the author does not interact with the audience, podcasts may be best utilized for promotional purposes. Currently, books cannot be purchased in the form of a podcast, but the author can always direct listeners to retail booksellers.

Online chats are also booming. Everywhere you turn, there is another chat provider. As an author, these ongoing forums can heighten awareness of your book. Because the same people often visit chat rooms repeatedly, if you can interest enough participants to comment, then you just might create a chain reaction for the sale of your book. Like podcasts, online chats are good promotional resources, but they still do not have the same impact that webinars or teleseminars have in terms of "selling" the author and his or her book, mainly due to the lack of interaction with the author.

More detailed information about the variety of social media outlets available for book-related events can be found in the "Online Promotion" chapter.

72 | Speaking Engagements Outside of Bookstores

Reach out to topic-specific groups, organizations, corporations, associations, clubs, schools, societies, museums, and charities that will benefit from an event with you and your book. These venues and organizations may be able to purchase books from the publisher at thirty-to-fifty percent off of the retail price. Discounts could be of interest to hosting venues that are looking to generate revenue from your appearance or to pass on savings to attendees.

Also, corporations might purchase a number of books to either resell or give away to attendees. If these copies are purchased from a retail outlet that reports to a bestseller list, then you might just get on the list!

Support your public event by sending out an email blast to friends, family members, and associates notifying them of your appearance and asking for their support in attending and buying a copy of your book. According to David Merman Scott, bestselling author of *The New Rules of Marketing & PR* and *World Wide Rave*, you need to inundate the marketplace. So, don't just send out one email blast; instead, send out multiple blasts containing different messages at different times of day over a period of time. He has proven that his methods work by promoting and publicizing his own book and eventually driving it to a bestseller ranking. Visit his website at davidmermanscott.com.

Try to have the hosting venue or organization purchase a set number of books (one hundred or more) in lieu of a speaker's fee. Depending on your usual fee, the venue will probably benefit more from purchasing discounted books than paying you directly, and you will benefit from the royalties generated by the sales of those copies.

Also consider creating your own workshop. Page Lambert, an author, editor, and lecturer, is forging her own road, combining her passions for the West and the great outdoors by organizing writer's retreats. Her openhearted approach to the writing life creates a safe passage for writers to explore their creativity. She's a mentor to every writer who has ever asked him or herself, "How can I write for a living and quit my day job?" Visit her website at pagelambert.com.

Whenever possible, whether you're appearing at a bookstore or some other live (or virtual) venue, arrange for book sales to count toward a bestseller list. Most bookstores and some non-brick and mortar stores (such as Amazon and Barnes & Noble Online) report to these coveted lists, but not all do, so be sure to ask before you decide who will be selling your book. This could be your shot at making the list!

73 | Teleseminars

In a teleseminar, the author addresses the audience via a phone line rather than in person. Like other speaking engagements, there is a fixed time frame during which the author's presentation and the audience's questions and answers will take place. The length of the talk can be as short or as long as you like, and audience size can vary from a very small number to thousands, depending on the capacity of the phone line being used.

Whether or not a teleseminar will be free to attendees depends on the host. Some organizations will charge the retail cost of the book, which guarantees that a certain number of books get sold, while others will not charge a fee, but will instead collect email addresses to which they can later send promotional materials soliciting the author's book or other support items for the sponsoring organization.

One of the major benefits to a teleseminar is that it requires no travel for either the author or the audience. For both the author and the audience, a teleseminar is accessible from home, office, or wherever else. To participate, audience members are given a phone number and an access code that allows them to log on to the presentation.

Many authors supplement their incomes through speaking engagements, which limits their available time. Because they tend to have heavy travel schedules, they may welcome the opportunity to stay at home, and the fact that teleseminar allows them to do so opens up an abundance of opportunities for the author to appear in front of his or her audience.

If desired, a teleseminar can be a DIY event thanks to online chat outlets such as messenger.yahoo.com, google.com/talk, msn.com, and skype.com. These chat clients put you in the driver's seat, but you also need to consider marketing your presentation.

If you don't have a substantial email list, try partnering with different organizations, clubs, associations, or businesses that have some connection to your niche audience. Utilizing their email lists and advertising your book with their products will be a win-win situation for everyone. It's also a good idea to check with your local library or bookstore about collaboration. Promoting the library or bookstore through your teleseminar could prove to be an added bonus, increasing their patronage and serving as a social reference for you. You become the company you keep.

74 | Webinars

Webinar author presentations are live events via the Internet in which participants can attend from home, the office, et cetera, and connect with you and other participants. In order to participate in a webinar, you will need a computer, an Internet connection, a telephone line, and/or a webcam. A webinar is either web-based, meaning attendees access it by entering an address into their web browsers, or is accessed through an application that is downloaded and saved to the computer's hard drive.

A webinar allows for interaction between the author and audience during a question-and-answer session. The author can also speak over the phone while pointing out information being shown on the computer screen.

There is webinar technology on the market that incorporates the use of audio equipment in order to allow for truly web-based communication (webex. com provides this kind of service). The costs of such services can range from a few hundred dollars to a few thousand, depending on bandwidth, number of participants, and whether or not you want the presentation archived for later use.

75 | Podcasts

Because podcast audiences are primarily listening audiences, podcasting is very similar to radio. The recording is downloaded to a computer or portable media player and enjoyed by fans at their own convenience. Besides audio, podcasts can also include video. In order to host your own podcast, you will need a computer, a microphone and headset, and software. The specifics of each component will vary depending on your budget and the quality that you wish to produce. There are many books about how to create podcasts, and *Podcasting for Dummies* and *PODCASTING: The Do-It-Yourself Guide* (Wiley) are great resources for everything you ever wanted to know about podcasting but were afraid to ask.

The good news is, podcasts are accessible and authors are using them to sell lots and lots of books. Podcasts are available through iTunes and you can make them available on your website. The beauty of this medium is that podcasts are portable and, because they are downloaded, are accessible from just about anywhere. A good podcaster has something interesting to say (your book is worth talking about, right?). Some authors have been able to develop their entire publicity campaigns around podcasts due to the ease with which book lovers can access them.

Podcast downloads have become popular topics of conversation at cocktail parties and, if you look carefully, you might see people listening to them while in line at the grocery store. How would you feel if you saw someone listening to one of your podcasts? (This could happen—remember to carry your book or a representation of your book with you at all times.)

A few years ago, roughly one percent of the computer-using population listened to podcasts regularly. That one percent amounted to about 320,000 people. Today, that percentage has grown to over twelve percent, amounting to about 1,320,000 people who habitually download and listen to podcasts.

Sounds like podcasts could be the next best thing to physically whispering your book's message into book lovers' ears.

76 | Electronic Readers

The Amazon Kindle is an e-book reader that uses an electronic paper display and system that reads only Kindle-formatted text. Anyone can upload an unpublished or self-published book to the Kindle list and name his or her own price. This is another way to gain exposure for your writing and it doesn't cost anything. If nothing else, it will allow you to see your work available on Amazon and might serve as a good ego boost. Announcing that your work is available as a Kindle edition on Amazon will draw additional readers to your writing and will provide you with a universal platform to which you can direct potential readers, editors, media, booksellers, and clients to your written work. The Sony Reader is an electronic book reader that is similar to the Kindle (sonystyle.com/reader).

Be advised that not all traditionally-published books are available in electronic format because they require specific production rights, which represent an added cost to the publisher. Ask your editor and review your contract to find out the terms applied to electronic rights of your book.

77 | Webcam Events

A great alternative to a webinar is a webcam author appearance. Creating author appearances has never been easier than turning on your computer, connecting to Skype or another live messenger provider, hooking up a webcam, and sending email invitations to a bookstore audience or conference. In a matter of minutes, you could be in front of a live audience of hundreds!

Skype is a great tool for hosting live author events via the Internet. Using a Logitech QuickCam Orbit AF with Skype, Windows Live Messenger, Yahoo! Messenger, AOL Instant Messenger (AIM), and other popular instant messaging applications will lead you to a new way of thinking about author appearances.

Establishing webcam events for authors is becoming more and more common. Wecbam author appearances between the publisher and the bookstore are sure to create a wave of authors clamoring for their publishers to get on board. This type of event creates all sorts of possibilities for bookstores, especially those located in the Midwest, as the number of authors who tour to that area is limited (traditionally, publishers are more likely to send authors to places like New York where national media is located).

Books can be made available to the in-store audience in three ways:

- Booksellers will have unsigned copies of the book in the store.
- The publisher will provide pre-signed copies of the book for the store to have on hand on the night of the event. A case of books will be sent to the author prior to the event to be signed and he or she will ship them to the bookstore.
- The author will have copies of the book at home that can be personalized for the attendees, just as would happen if the author were physically in the bookstore. The webcam will be stationed in the store, and the customer will come to the author's virtual table and greet him or her face-to-face over the Internet. They can exchange greetings and the author will sign the customer's books and ship them to the bookstore, where the customer will retrieve the prepaid, personalized, autographed copies.

It's a win-win for everyone! More books get to more people and the author's audience continues to expand.

78 | Online Chat

Authors can chat online about their books with individual fans or groups. Online chatting has been popular for some time and continues to gain momentum as a great platform for book promotion. Below are a few groups that you might want to think about joining:

- online-tech-tips.com
- groups.msn.com
- chatmaker.net

Creating your own chat based on your book will allow you to explore an infinite number of possible outlets for the sale of your book and possible speaking opportunities, as the outreach is determined by your guest list, word of mouth, links, and promotion. Be adventurous, research groups, and join discussions in which you can introduce yourself and your book. Facebook, MySpace, LinkedIn, and other social networking sites all have chat sections. You might just be surprised at how receptive people will be when they hear that you're an author.

79 | Second Life, YouTube, Facebook, and MySpace

These social media outlets are leading the way to a whole new virtual world for authors and their fans. You have to experience them to believe it.

One of the most bizarre social media sites is Second Life, a three-dimensional, virtual world created by its residents (secondlife.com). There are even resident authors making real money through virtual bookstore appearances and sales of their books. Publishers have set up shop, too—you can pitch your manuscript to a virtual editor. It's just unbelievable! Second Life can also host meetings, chats, and press conferences. It's free!

YouTube is a website that allows users to upload, view, and share video clips (youtube.com). Authors and publishers are uploading "book trailers," which are interviews and audio-visual snippets of books. Video-recorded book talks are also made available to millions of viewers. All of this exposure translates to more readers for your book. Make sure that your book appears in every video clip you upload, along with a message to the viewers telling them where they can purchase the book. YouTube boasts millions of video uploads with millions of global viewers, with numbers increasing daily.

Facebook (facebook.com) is a social networking site on which authors can join networks organized by city, workplace, school, and region to connect with potential readers of their book. Because of the global impact of Facebook, publishers are using it to launch book campaigns. Authors can add friends, family members, and whomever else they wish to notify about their book. Authors are using Facebook to post video logs about their books, invitations to appearances, and updates as to what they're working on currently. Many fans and readers are responding with delight at the chance to actually see and hear their favorite authors and to discover new authors. Take a look for yourself to see the number of authors who are represented.

On Facebook, posting an entry to your profile or to someone else's profile automatically sends a notification to all of your friends and to the friends of the person on whose page you posted, thereby connecting you and your friends to friends of your friends.

MySpace is another popular, interactive social networking website. It's another place to promote your book to hundreds of thousands of people and, like all of the other social networks, it's free! (myspace.com.)

80 | Flickr, LinkedIn, Twitter, and Internet Cafes

Flickr (flickr.com) is an image and video hosting online community. Authors use Flickr to showcase book tour photos and upload videos. As of November 2008, it claimed to host more than three billion images. While Flickr is a visual hosting service, authors can list upcoming book-related appearances, photos from prior speaking engagements, commentary, and book cover images. As the saying goes, "A picture is worth a thousand words."

LinkedIn (linkedin.com) is a business-oriented social networking site that is used by authors to connect with anyone in business who may be interested in their books. As of December 2007, the site was visited by 3.2 million people every month, an increase of 485% from the end of 2006. As of October 2008, it had more than thirty million registered users spanning 150 industries. Authors are using LinkedIn to gain exposure and to grow their networks of followers. *It's all grist for the mill.*

Twitter (twitter.com) is another site that can link you to the virtual world of social networking. Twitter posts, or "tweets," can consist of a maximum of 140 characters. An author can give a blow-by-blow, real time description of working on his or her novel, preparing for an upcoming media appearance, or walking into a live appearance. Publicists are also tweeting about their authors and thus heightening the media's attention and response. The instantaneous nature of Twitter is very exciting because there are no retakes—it's all about now. Being live in real time can turn into book sales or media attention in the moment.

In the book, *Twitter Power: How to Dominate Your Market One Tweet at a Time*, by Joel Comm (Wiley), Comm suggests that businesses are using Twitter to interact with customers and other businesses in a whole new way. Comm sees Twitter and other social media outlets as means toward building customer following, expanding brands, and generating buzz through its integration with existing marketing strategies.

Whether you join all or one of these social networks, being involved and seen online in these forums is a must and will undoubtedly produce book sales. These growing mediums for promoting and announcing your book to targeted audiences and communities are unique in that the audiences are built-in, as members log on regularly to check out the newest updates.

At an internet cafe (or cyberspace cafe), customers pay a per minute, per hour, or other fee to use a computer with Internet access. The customer can enjoy having food and drink brought directly to the table, giving him or her the freedom to write uninterrupted. Internet cafes might seem a bit off-the-beaten-path as a means toward book promotion, but keep in mind that many authors have utilized them to write great novels. For example, J.K. Rowling, one of the most famous authors in the world, wrote the majority of the first of the *Harry Potter* series in a cafe.

To understand the advantages of sitting among strangers versus sitting in your comfy writer's studio with all its amenities, you'll just have to give cafes a try. Being in a new environment may allow you to go deeper into yourself in a way that you've not experienced before. You might be able to tune out the crowd and the noise of the espresso machine and just listen to your inner voice, loud and clear. Sometimes, depending on what you're writing, giving your mind's gatekeeper something else to focus on will give you direct access to your inner knowing and voice. It's really amazing!

Promoting your writing at these cafes is usually an easy task. The purveyors are happy to have you drink their coffee all day, and your presence will bring a certain mystique or cache to the establishment and magnetically draw people to sit for a while. Have your business cards, current book, or mock-up of the book jacket with you and leave it in open sight. You might just attract a member of the local media who happens to have stopped in for a cup of java. At the very least, you'll probably be asked if you're a writer, which will open up a conversation about your book and where the customer will be able to purchase it.

81 | Media Bistro and Craigslist

Authors and those in or interested in publishing gather around the water cooler through a website called MediaBistro (mediabistro.com), which publishes various blogs and job listings for journalists and publishing professionals. It was originally targeted toward professionals in New York City but has since grown into an international resource with almost a million registered users. Among the services offered by the site are job listings, educational courses, forums, events, and its premium subscription service, Avant-Guild. The site also hosts many industry-specific blogs, including TVNewser (which covers broadcast and cable news), GalleyCat (book publishing), UnBeige (design), AgencySpy (advertising), PRNewser (public relations), and Mobile Content Today (mobile apps). These blogs present authors with a unique opportunity to plug their books in a place where almost a million viewers gather—what a plethora of information, opportunity, and contacts for every author!

MediaBistro also publishes FishBowl blogs, which reveal journalism gossip centric to New York, Los Angeles, and DC. What a great way to get insider information about who's coming and going to and from one publishing house or the next. You might also just pick up an agent or publisher by working in a mention about your book in a comment on a FishBowl blog.

MediaBistro is a great resource for writing courses, freelance and full-time writing jobs, and keeping pace with who's in the limelight. Authors can also find the answers to questions such as, who's publishing who's book? What was the purchase price? and How many books is the publisher predicting that they will print?

Craigslist is an online classifieds site that has several different categories that authors are using to promote their books. The great thing about Craigslist is that an author can promote regionally, state-by-state, or country-by-country, which allows him or her to focus on his or her core demographic. When you pitch your book to readers who are drawn to your subject matter, you quicken the pace of the book's sales.

Some categories that make sense for an author's book promotion include:

- Community
- Discussion forums
- For sale
- Services
- Gigs

All of these categories have sub-categories in which authors can list upcoming appearances and offer their books for sale. The national and international capabilities of Craigslist make this medium very appealing, and it's also free. Have a look at craigslist.org/about.

82 | Social Media

Social media refers to Internet and mobile-based tools for sharing and discussing information—in this case, your book. The term suggests interaction through the use of integrated technology, telecommunications, social interaction, and the construction of words, pictures, video, and audio.

Social media venues include:

- Blogs
- Microblogs (Twitter)
- Social networking (Facebook, LinkedIn, MySpace)
- Photo sharing (Flickr)
- Video sharing (YouTube)
- Audio/music sharing (iTunes)
- Virtual worlds (Second Life)

So, how do you choose the best ones for the promotion of your book? Each one has a feasible platform for most books and require time for setup, interaction, and regular updates in order to collect the benefits. Which ones will work best for you are determined by your individual preference and what you feel makes sense for your book. Do your research to figure out where you will maximize your efforts and turn your time into book sales.

83 | Search Engine Optimization (SEO) and Keywords

Search engine optimization, or SEO, is the process of making the pages of a website more easily reached and searched by search engine spiders so that it will attract visitors by achieving top ranking on major search engines for selected keyword phrases. Keyword strength is vital to the success and return on your investment for your website, blog, or other online outlet. By paying attention to SEO, sales success through your website or blog is likely. Visit seologic.com for more information.

Keyword density is important and refers to the number of times a keyword or key phrase appears in relation to the total number of words on a page. In terms of SEO, keyword density helps determine whether a website is relevant to a specific keyword or phrase. The use of keywords will directly determine the number of hits you receive for your website or blog. For more information, visit keyworddensity.com.

84 | Electronic Press Kit (EPK)

An electronic press kit is, as the name would suggest, a press kit in electronic form. They are used to promote authors via mass electronic media and can be distributed through several channels, including:

- powerpresskits.com
- newswire.com
- email blast
- your website or blog

An EPK can also be used to contact speaking venues, which expedites the response time for scheduling an appearance.

85 | Long Tail

The term "Long Tail" was coined by Chris Anderson in an article that appeared in the October 2004 issue of *Wired Magazine*. The term describes the niche strategy of businesses that sell large numbers of unique items in relatively small quantities.

How does this concept relate to you and your book? Well, most bookstores, both brick and mortar and online, are practicing this strategy in their businesses. Because the markup on books is minimal, retailers look for other means to increase their profit margins. Selling ancillary products such as gift items, apparel, specialty foods, picture frames, reading glasses, bookends, et cetera, all help to support the bookstore that is selling your book. For this reason, you might want to consider creating a gift item to sell in conjunction with your book. For example. children's book authors sometimes have dolls, stuffed toys, or other gizmos packaged with their books. Culinary authors might include cooking utensils with theirs. These extras serve to attract extra attention to books. A good example of a gift item added to a book is the *Pat the Bunny* and plush bunny package by Dorothy Kunhardt. The book can be purchased with or without the stuffed bunny and actually became a bestseller prior to this rendition.

Be aware, however, that gift items represent an added cost for the publisher and can create challenges in terms of merchandising your book in the bookstore. Bookshelves are designed to hold books, and when a book is packaged with another item, the store has to find another place to stock it, which takes it away from the shelf on which it would normally be located. Do your homework before launching into creating a clever gadget that may end up doing more harm than good. Most importantly, the book should be able to stand on it's own. The gift item is just that—an add-on.

86 | Electronic Book Images

The days when text files, photos, and artwork were handled in hard copy form are going by the wayside. Unless you're creating a one-of-a-kind, handmade book, your book's content will be produced and reproduced electronically. This allows for swift transfer of the book to the printer, and any necessary adjustments can be handled more easily.

A jpeg file is a common method of compressing photographic images. The degree of compression can be adjusted, allowing a selectable trade off between storage size and image quality. A jpeg usually achieves 10:1 compression with little perceptible loss in image quality. Book covers and other interior photos and artwork are typically produced in jpeg format for reproduction on the book's jacket (front or back) and for use on the publisher's, bookstore's, or author's websites.

A tif file is a tagged image file used by publishers for storing photographs and art to be used for scanning, faxing, word processing, and other applications. Publishers also use tif files for page layouts.

The Internet offers more promotional opportunities to connect with readers than ever before. New social media venues continue to pop up and beckon you to join them and the technical tools within and around the available applications are staggering.

87 | Author's Website

Having your own website helps to make your book available to a massive amount of outlets, including bookstores, organizations, libraries, museums, and clubs that may be interested in selling your book and/or hosting an appearance with you.

Don't worry if you're not tech-savvy. There are website builders that are easily navigated with point-and-click direction. Creating a website can be simple and doesn't have to cost a lot of money. Many template-oriented website providers make the process of establishing yourself on the web simple and affordable. A few examples are register.com, homestead.com, and web.com. If cost is an issue, then there are many free website building services out there that are worth exploring. A great free resource is freewebs.com. Check out theartandbusinessofwriting.com for an example of what this resource can offer.

An author's website is a convenient way to display limited content of your book and biographical information and to build an email list of interested visitors for your current and future books. Websites allow the media to look at your book and background and help them to decide whether or not to interview you.

You can sell your book directly from your website or direct visitors to a local, national, or other bookseller. Your website will allow your readers to get to know you in-depth, which will increase your readership, and including a blog will also help to increase your following.

88 | Blogging

The blog (short for "web log") is becoming a leading method of generating media attention, promotion, and sales. A blog differs from a website in that it is updated regularly and acts as an online record of an author's goings-on. In some respects, blogging is replacing the need to have a website. Establishing a blog based on your book and its message will allow you to link to other pertinent blogs, receive comments, and acquire vendor's support in the way of advertising sponsorship.

The positive impact of having a blog and/or website is measurable, as you can track hits, ask for feedback (in the form of comments), and receive ratings from visitors. If you're curious about the hits that a blog is receiving, sign up for an RSS feed (which stands for Really Simply Syndication) and receive daily updates.

You can also list your blog on Technorati (technorati. com/ping) and Google (blogsearch.google.com/ping). Do your own research on how your blog is faring among others—it's very exciting!

Blogs can be produced through services such as blogger.com/home, radio.userland.com, or typepad.com for free.

Blogging about your book or topic on other related blogs can also generate traffic for your blog and site. As a marketing strategy, blogging will increase an author's profile and draw attention to his or her book. Blogs are also great for compiling email lists.

While a website enables you to have a global reach and connect with other sites that may support your book, a blog is able to cast a broader net and catch notice from viewers who might not have had any curiosity about your website or book had it not been for the angle or spin presented in a blog. Direct readers to an excerpt from your book, a review, or an interview by posting a mention that your book on a particular subject is now available. Be sure to include the publisher's name and where the book can be purchased.

For more information on how to blog, *Blogging for Dummies* and *Buzz Marketing for Dummies*, both published by Wiley, are good resources.

89 | Email Blasts

An email blast is an email message that contains a number (at least two or more) of recipients. The purpose of an email blast is to contact a large number of people who may be interested in what you have written all at once. It saves the author time in reaching out to readers, speaking venues, and the media.

Do some research and make a list of potential audiences for your topic. For example, if you're writing a book about bicycling through wine country, look for wineries and cycling groups in the locales addressed in your book. Compile an email list and run a test to check the accuracy of the email addresses.

Now is not the time to be shy about asking your friends and family for help. More than likely, they have an email address list that they could use to send a message about your book. If they're receptive, coordinate your email blasts in order to maximize the impact. Email blasts in support of your book sent by friends and family act as social proof of your authority.

Buying an email list related to your book's topic is advantageous and can certainly generate sales, but make sure that your messages won't be recognized as spam by the recipients' mail or anti-virus software. Creating an effective message for the subject line of the email is one key element to its success.

An email blast should include:

- Greeting
- Personalized message
- Invitation to view your website, blog, or social media profiles

- Mention of your book, the topic, and information on where to purchase it
- Personal closing
- Salutation
- Your name, book title, publisher, ISBN, and a link to an online bookseller.

These days, most authors have their own email lists that they continually update with new addresses that they've collected through their websites, blogs, or social networking profiles.

If you're unable to send email blasts yourself due to limitations set forth by your ISP (Internet Service Provider), there are services that can assist you, including netatlantic.com, icontact.com, and e-mailblasters.com.

Be sure to alert your editor with information about the timing of your email announcements so that he or she can notify the sales force. This will ensure that books will be available at all of the bookselling outlets.

90 | An Author's Time Management

Determining what works best for you and your book is an ongoing process that will always be a part of your book's campaign and your writing. If you try to be everywhere, you might lose impact, because each site, blog, chat, and so on requires your time. Then again, the ability to be everywhere is the gift of the Internet.

So what is an author to do? If you're in a position to hire an administrative manager for your web presence, you might be able to spread your message on a wider scale; however, some of your time will still be required to develop your comments, content, or messages for updates. On the other hand, if you're the author and the administrator of your website, blog, chats, and social media profiles, then you could get overwhelmed, which could result in a lack of consistency.

In both scenarios, though, aren't you also busy writing another book, essay, article, or column? Maybe you have a day job. You're in a writers' group, attending writers' conferences, and reading writing magazines. You're blogging, linking, and posting comments on other blogs and websites. How do you find the time to do all of this and support your book?

Time is one of the biggest issues that we all have to manage. At the beginning of the social media explosion, some authors tried to have it all, contributing to writer-centric sites, blogs, and chats whenever a new one cropped up. It's important to take an assessment of your open time and use what you have efficiently.

Trackbacks, pingbacks, and tweets, oh my! Will there ever be an end to the newfangled things to be used to earn the attention of the majority? Probably not. One of the most important things to do is to form relationships with people who are interested in topics similar to that of your book. Research the marketplace and establish bonds with related readers through social media outlets.

91 | Repetition

While this book has covered publicity, marketing, and events and discussed the importance of all of these promotional outlets, the real necessity of repetition has yet to be discussed in-depth. How much of all of the above and other components of the book's campaign does it take to hit a bestseller list? If a crystal ball were an option, then this question would have a definitive answer; however, what is being shared with you comes from fifteen years of experience.

As Tony Robbins once said in a live Master Class in Hawaii, "Repetition is the mother of skill." What did he mean by this? The word mother brings to mind someone who has a lot of experience, insight, and courage to lead the way. How does this relate to your book campaign? Developing a skill is a particular expertise, and we develop skill by doing the same thing over and over again. So, if you want to be the "mother" of your book campaign and increase your chances of hitting a bestseller list, whether it be regional or national, consider practicing the tips that are covered in this section and anything else that comes to mind over and over again.

92 | Effective Advertising Steps

It's as easy as counting to five:

1. Get noticed
2. Bond with the reader
3. Present a compelling reason to buy
4. Tell the reader *why* they must have your book
5. Get the reader to take action, NOW—create a sense of urgency.

It's important to follow the order of the steps in the advertising process. Try to think of yourself as the customer and consider what has gotten your attention in the past and caused you to buy; this may offer you a clue as to how to go about presenting your book to potential buyers.

93 | Email Blasts

Create a list of email addresses for your book campaign to be delivered at specific times of the day on specific days of the week or month. Here are some things to keep in mind:

- Your subject line makes a difference as to whether or not your email will be opened by the receiver.

- If you send your message too many times in a given period of time, it may be viewed as spam by the recipient and/or the recipient's server. It doesn't take much to understand that, just like junk mail in your home or office mailbox, after you've received the same piece of advertising with the same look and feel over and over again, you know the message. If the sender's declaration failed to get your attention from the beginning, chances are you're not going to give it any notice.

- Direct toward your niche audience: The beauty of email blasts is you can actually control who reads your message. Unlike advertising that falls on deaf ears, to a degree, you can direct your message to your niche audience. Hitting the target audience for your book will expedite your results.

- You will know who opened your email, how many opened it, and, depending how you direct your responses, you will know if they took action.

Recommended reading:

- *Email Marketing* by Jeanniey Mullen and David Daniels (Wiley, 2009)

- *Email Marketing by the Numbers* by Chris Baggott with Ali Sales (Wiley, 2007).

94 | Links

Posting links to your website and/or blog on other related sites and blogs furthers your chances of being noticed. In other words, you're not waiting for readers to visit your sites, but you're proactively going to where the readers are congregating.

95 | Media Appearances

The press holds the keys to the city of bookselling. If you want to be a bestselling author, you have to generate publicity. As was discussed earlier, there is never too much publicity—the more, the better. Take the risk of sending your press release to anyone who could be interested in your topic; however, be careful not to send it to press that has absolutely nothing to do with your subject matter or has passed on your previous queries on this topic.

Remember, earlier in the release of your book is optimum timing. The longer your book is on the shelf, the less likely it is that the media will show interest.

96 | Events

Any opportunity you get to speak about your book, take it! Unlike press appearances, speaking to a live audience or virtual audience will ensure that your book will be in favor for a long time.

97 | Can You Make The "List"?

In his book, *Making the List* (Barnes & Noble, 2001), Michael Korda points out that a book that makes the list isn't necessarily noteworthy—that, in fact, many books that end up on bestseller lists surprise both the authors and the publishers. While authors and publishers have attempted to come up with a formula for making it to a bestseller list, no one has figured out how to make it happen repeatedly. Some believe that it's a matter of having a book published within a particular time frame, in a number of reporting stores, and in mass quantities. While this method has been successful for some books, it's still not a proven way to make a bestseller. Some authors have tried purchasing bulk numbers of books through bookstores or other reporting retail outlets in a specific number of hours and on the same day. Yes, this has proven successful for some, but it's not effective every time. There are just too many factors to consider, including competing books and their promotional efforts, current events that make certain books more or less appealing, book-store shelf placement, the book's release time, and so much more.

Daily promotion within the first six weeks of your book's pub window will drive hundreds, maybe thousands, to notice your book. It's all about being noticed, but it's important to be noticed by the right people (the right people being members of the media, book retail outlets, and book-buying customers).

98 | Social Media

Exhaust ALL social media outlets, even those that you think may not be worthwhile. In the end, they all feed off of one another.

99 | How Do I Get People to Recommend My Book?

How do you get people to refer your book to their friends, family members, and colleagues? Word of mouth has proven to be one of the most effective forms of promotion. Among your inner circle, who has read your book? Give your book away and it will come back ten times in sales.

100 | Where is the Heart in my Book's Message?

Creating a sincere, heartfelt message about your book's topic and a compelling reason that people must buy it is necessary. By getting in touch with the readers' emotions, you will influence them to open their wallets. For the most part, people base their actions on their emotions, rather than on what their minds say.

101 | Adding Value to Your Published Book

What else can you sell or give away in conjunction with your book?

Do you have something that can be paired with your book? What if you've written a scary children's story and one of the characters is a cute, but ugly, monster? Packaging the book with the toy monster will undoubtedly increase sales. Think about what item or service you can box up with your book.

More Titles in the LifeTips Book Series

101 MORTGAGES TIPS
by Bill Pirraglia

101 SUCCESSFUL PR CAMPAIGN TIPS
by Mary White

101 NATURAL HEALTHY EATING TIPS
by Emily Davidson

101 GREEN TRAVEL TIPS
by Lydia Handiak